THE PERVERSE ORGANISATION
AND ITS DEADLY SINS

THE PERVERSE ORGANISATION AND ITS DEADLY SINS

Susan Long

KARNAC

First published in 2008 by
Karnac Books Ltd
118 Finchley Road, London NW3 5HT

British Library Cataloguing in Publication Data
A C.I.P for this book is available from the British Library

ISBN-13: 978–1–85575–576–5

Edited, designed, and produced by
Florence Production Ltd, Stoodleigh, Devon
www.florenceproduction.co.uk

Printed in Great Britain
www.karnacbooks.com

CONTENTS

ABOUT THE AUTHOR

Susan Long, PhD, is Professor of Creative and Sustainable Organizations at Royal Melbourne Institute of Technology University, Australia. She is editor of *Socio-Analysis*, past President of the International Society for the Psychoanalytic Study of Organizations and President of Group Relations Australia.

PREFACE

A colleague said to me that he has heard too much about corruption in organisations and would rather hear of more hopeful organisational stories. I share the desire for a hopeful future. But, I believe that hope arises from a position of squarely facing the current situation and its difficulties. We still have much to learn about organisations, how they operate and the effect they have on us. My interest is in the ways that humans act unconsciously and collectively. Although corrupt behaviour is often consciously planned and executed, it most often occurs against a background of less than conscious cultural assumptions and collusions. It is these that may form a perverse culture.

In my day to day life I am an ordinary product of my society. I see myself as an individual with my own thoughts and ambitions; my own needs and frailties. I desire the comforts offered by my culture, I enjoy the entertainments provided, the intellectual challenges that I can find. I grumble about many things that dissatisfy. Along with my neighbours, I am a consumer. In all this, I am embedded. Also, I am very curious about how the culture around me has made me what I am. How it is that I share assumptions with my friends and colleagues and am driven by collective attitudes and perspectives. When I explore this, sometimes I am shocked at the "taken-for-granteds" around me, while feeling powerless to bring about change—even within myself. The issues of global climate change and terrorism, for example, come to mind. When in this position I could withdraw, even turn a blind eye, or I can attempt to understand, perhaps even to act upon my understanding.

Humans have both selfish and communal desires. As has always been the case, we need each other. This means that sometimes we use and abuse each other, while at other times we are capable of transcending our selfishness. Perverse patterns of behaviour involve more than individual selfishness, however. In this book, I have looked at perversity as a social phenomenon, as a cultural pattern. My curiosity about perversity comes from many sources. In the early years of my career I was a psychotherapist. Sometimes I came in contact with people whose behaviour was quite perverse. As a psychoanalytic psychotherapist, I was curious about and studied the nature of perversity in individuals from the different theoretical perspectives of the Kleinians and the Lacanians. In the late 1990s and early 2000s I did research in the Victorian Justice system, that led me to do field work at a specialised prison for sex offenders. The whole question as to whether these offenders were "bad" or "mad" was evident. The organisational system designed to contain them was conflicted around this question. Finally, as the mother of adolescent sons, I was briefly exposed to the music of some heavy metal rock groups whose lyrics seemed both creative and often perverse. The general culture seemed more open to allow for perversity.

My background in psychoanalysis, together with my work in management education led me to think about organisations and the, at times, seeming madness within them. I became involved in "Group Relations" which is a field of endeavour dedicated to the study of conscious and unconscious psychodynamics within groups and organisations. The idea that organisations are sites of collective defences against anxiety, depression, guilt and other emotions and that these defences unconsciously structure the organisation, threw light on a multitude of experiences.

I had been thinking through the differences between madness in individuals and madness in organisations when the story of Enron broke into the news. My thinking was leading me to see organisations as systems of agreements between people. The medical model of madness was not quite right. Things go wrong in social systems when agreements are broken, connections are not made, roles and boundaries are confused, authority is abused, consultation is absent, when the "right hand" does not know what the "left hand" is doing or when information is confused, ignored or absent. We think of these things happening when the right organisational systems have not been developed or are not correctly in place. True, but why has this occurred? It is through the presence of complex human emotions and group dynamics. For example, someone or some group has not been called to account. Communication has failed because "in-the-mind" one group didn't count and was missed out. The CEO fails to see the significance of a piece of information because he or she is intent on seeing something else. With Enron, I began to see perversity rather than psychosis (madness). The conscious corruption was evident in the cover-up stories, but on closer examination I could see the presence of collective perversity. What is meant by this is described in the book, but for now it is sufficient to say that the individuals were neither mad nor perverse. It was the culture that showed much evidence of perversity. I wrote a paper on this. Michael Long (Mike) my husband then introduced me to the book *Inventing Money* by Nicholas Dunbar, suggesting to me that Long-Term Capital Management (LTCM), the company described there might be a case of perverse pride. By then, the idea for this book became firm.

In this book I focus on perverse organisations. I don't infer that all organisations have perverse cultures, although I suspect the potential is always there. I define and explore what a perverse culture is and how it becomes manifest in a variety of organisations. Since beginning my exploration, many of my students have reported aspects of organisational culture that fit the picture I give and their reports encouraged me to write.

I thank Mike for his encouragement and support, not least of which was to help me in the final editing. I also thank colleagues John Newton and James Krantz for reading the manuscript and giving me feedback. Thanks to Wendy Harding and Mike Faris for their encouragement and support at RMIT University. The book builds on my thinking over the years. This has been supported by many people, too numerous to mention here but including colleagues from the International Society for the Psychoanalytic Study of Organisations, The Australian Institute of Socio-Analysis (now closed), Group Relations Australia, The Tavistock Institute of Human Relations and other group relations organisations internationally, and Victoria University, Swinburne and RMIT Universities in Melbourne. Thanks to my students who always provide stimulation of thinking through discussions and their own work, and to all those in the organisations that have been part of my research. Thanks to my now adult children, Tamsenne, Jason and Cable for their support of me in my work.

CHAPTER ONE

The Perverse Organisation

The idea of perversion conjures up many images of dark and sinister practices; evil and sadistic; masochistic and filled with secret lust; trespass into forbidden places, dungeons and hidden lairs; not a part of everyday life. Yet, small perverse acts and intentions are a constant part of the social psychological landscape. There is the sadism of the office bully who gains pleasure from the discomfort of others; the fetishistic attraction of consumerism and commodification, with their endless quest for more, never quite satisfying so rapaciously creating new and better markets; the suicidal backdrop of substance abuse and workaholism, out of control; and the voyeuristic pleasures found in the culture of celebrity which acts as a substitute for real intimacy. Good and bad, the presence and effects of perverse dynamics are an integral part of our culture and imbued within our working lives. This book will examine the nature of perversity and its presence in collective corporate and organisational life.

There is evidence of a movement from a culture of narcissism[1] towards elements of a perverse culture.[2] This book will bring forth and examine that evidence as it reveals itself through one of the major institutions of our time—the work organisation. Corporations and organisations for work, production and service are major centres of social activity. In many senses they provide a critical source of identity for their members, just as do families and religions. Their examination gives access to most of the dynamics operating within our society and reveals some of the deeper assumptions upon which

1

our lives are based. To call them simply a reflection of human social organisation and proclivity, perhaps, is to underrate their importance in shaping today's psyche. To look at the formation of perverse practice, structure and culture within organisations is also to look at that development in society more broadly.

The narcissism and individualism present in late twentieth-century establishment has, through its values of self, greed, consumerism, acquisition and exploitation, promoted the emergence of perversion through the process of turning a blind eye.[3] This is relevant to, and has an effect on organisational life. Unconscious perverse dynamics become more evident, as do the conscious accompaniments of corruption. Perversion and corruption are not the same and, in respect to examining organisational life, we are more familiar with the idea of conscious corruption. But, the two are often linked as in those cases where, for instance, organisation leaders attempt to cover up perceived failures in an attempt to manipulate the share market and provide leverage for a hoped for recovery. The denial involved in turning a blind eye can become a conscious attempt to disguise a reality all too evident. The psychological dynamics of corruption are manifest in "greed, arrogance, a sense of personal entitlement, the idea of virtue as personal loyalty, and the inability to distinguish between organisational and personal ends".[4] The personal and organisational personae displayed through such characteristics as these are the eventual outcomes of an unconscious perverse societal dynamic. Perverse dynamics eventually lead to corrupt behaviours within the system.

The Deadly Sins of Organisations

Manifestations of perversity in organisations and corporations, I call the deadly sins of organisations because, when evidenced in ways that dominate the organisation's culture or "character", they are destructive. Regarding an organisation as having character is quite a step beyond the ideas of corporate culture made popular since the 1980s where corporate culture was simply defined as "the way things are done"?[5]: a kind of collective set of learned habits, attitudes, values and ways of thinking. Character, psychopathic or otherwise, is more deeply engrained and infers a more firmly established collectivity, as if the company has a mind of its own, together with attendant emotions. The idea of a corporation or organisation being swamped by particular emotions, thoughts and desires that become akin to character traits is implicit in this view. Leaving aside for now the full question of the possibility of the "character of an organisation" and how individuals are related to, or are a part of this, I shall propose the idea that organisations and corporations may *seem* to have character and beg my reader to stay with such an idea for the present. For, if the organisation is a piece of social reality constructed *in-the-mind* as much as in bricks and mortar, then *in-the-mind* it may have character as much as any other social construction, such as "mother" or "the police" or "a manager". That is, we may experience the organisation as an entity with volition and character and behave with this in mind.

By seeing the organisation as imbued with character, I shall explore the way certain organisational character traits inform the actions taken by organisational leaders and members. Many such character traits may, of course, foster corporate growth. However, when other destructive traits dominate the actions of organisational members from within an unconsciously perverse social structure, we can regard them as corporate sins.

The following chapters look at various forms of perversity as they appear in organisations. My basic argument is that organised corporate corruption is a conscious manifestation, the iceberg tip of an unconscious perverse societal structure and dynamic. Corruption builds on an underlying social fabric of perversity. But, conscious corruption is not the only manifestation of collective perversity. Other manifestations within various forms of organisation also need to be examined.

Although many people work in small businesses and not-for-profit organisations, the large corporate form is a modern archetype that has deeply influenced other forms of organisation. "Corporatisation" is highly valued and has become equivalent to being "business-like". Bakan's book and then film *The Corporation*[6] took as its theme: 1) the idea of the corporation created as a legal entity similar to an individual in the law; and, following this, 2) the evaluation of the behaviour of corporations against descriptions of psychopathic syndromes in the DSM IV, the recognised handbook of psychiatric nosology. The conclusion was that many corporations are psychopathic. Does this conclusion seem extreme? Perhaps it only fits some cases? But, such extreme manifestations as referred to in the book and film are extensions of practices that are in fact within the limits of the law, part and parcel of how we believe business should operate. In accepting them we may have become acclimatised to perverse practice.

There are very real differences between different forms of work organisation, for example, corporation or non-corporatised small business; bureaucracy or association; private or listed companies. Nonetheless, each contains people who collectively give rise to similar psychosocial dynamics. It is these psychosocial dynamics and their systemic causes that will be explored. Corporations, as depicted in the film and book of that name are a special form of organisation. They allow collective ownership through shareholding and, since the middle of the nineteenth century, have a limited liability form so that shareholders are not liable for company debts. This structure gives the corporation the status of an individual in the law.

> By the end of the nineteenth century, through a bizarre legal alchemy courts had fully transformed the corporation into a "person", with its own identity, separate from the flesh-and-blood people who were its owners and managers and empowered, like a real person to conduct business in its own name, acquire assets, employ workers, pay taxes, and go to court to assert its rights and defend its actions.[7]

This institutional form has had far-reaching effects on our work lives. Despite the fact that small privately owned businesses and not-for-profit organisations employ a large percentage of the workforce, the corporate form has come to dominate the way we understand business. For example, the separation of ownership, governance and management born in the early days of corporate history, provides a general model of business functioning even in organisational forms such as partnerships. Bakan argues that because the corporate form allows for a multitude of widely dispersed owners unable realistically to collaborate, except where the owners are other corporations—and these may be highly competitive—it becomes divorced from those individuals. In a life of its own, it has a "legally defined mandate to pursue, relentlessly, and without exception, its own self-interest, regardless of the often harmful consequences it might cause to others".[8] Corporate power is immense, especially in its multinational form. Its influence on all forms of work organisation, via its culture and business dominance is insidious. Through many real-life examples, Bakan argues the case for the pathological nature of corporations, their ability to "externalize" their effects so that outsiders suffer, their capacity to evade external regulation, and, through capital and influence, to ensure that government regulation is diminished. Dominated by a powerful elite of managers, largely beyond any control of small shareholders, modern corporations are compelled to be ruthless, despite the humanity and regardless of the personalities of those in the management roles. Even their attempted "good works" in the long run often suit the aim of increasing profits.[9] That is their very nature within capitalism.

Bakan's analysis is essentially political. The modern multinational corporation is a juggernaut with dynamics extending out from its political mandate. His suggestions are to strengthen external regulation, ensuring that self-regulation is not primary, to strengthen political democracy so that governments actually do regulate rather than "partner" industry, and to create a robust public sphere.[10] But, disturbing as his analysis is, is a political analysis enough? How can we understand the hidden psychological dimension that propels us in the first place to create and give birth to the pathological institution described by Bakan, that so dominates all of our current organisational forms?

This book looks less at a political/economic analysis and more at understanding the perverse dynamics underlying the political surface. It examines the nature of perversion as a basic human phenomenon and how the dynamics of perversion may be established in organisations. Bakan gives some hints. The institution of the corporation has become divided from the humans who populate it. In becoming a legal person in itself, set apart from those who own and populate it through limited liability and anonymous shareholding, it has managed to move away from human ethics, feelings and responsibilities. Indeed, the people who work within the corporations are left to hold (or not hold) the ethics, feelings and responsibilities, that the corporation itself does not. Often corporate or organisation members in their private lives carry personal anxieties and misgivings about how they are compelled to act in their working roles. I argue that the process goes beyond the "division" that Bakan suggests. Many of the thoughts and feelings that the workplace engenders are unconsciously projected into the corporation that then acts them out through corporate roles, sometimes against the conscious inclinations of the private individual. This demonstrates the effects of psychological denial and splitting at a societal level. Such institutional level dynamics are carried also into non-corporatised organisations and our everyday life.

In conducting an examination of the perverse nature of organisations, support will be drawn from social theories, depth psychology, psychoanalysis and concepts about human systems. Depth psychology and psychoanalysis provide an understanding of the inner life of a person. Here, character is regarded as influenced by inner forces that drive and shape thoughts, feelings and behaviours. How the person reacts to and makes sense of their inner life and social environment is also part of their character. In this book, psychology and psychoanalytic thinking will be applied to the organisation as a whole, or sub-parts of the organisation.

Systems thinking provokes the idea that the individual psyche is just one element in, or part of, a broader system of human culture, itself having "character". Discovering those aspects of a social system that represent a collective "inner life" is the work of systems psychodynamics[11] or socio-analysis. I take here what might be seen as an eclectic approach within systems psychodynamics, using arguments derived from several theories. While I understand that many theories have conflicting conceptual schemas, the task I set myself in this book is not to argue or attempt to resolve those more academic conflicts. It is to present a coherent picture of the emerging perverse culture evident in organisations, drawing from the work of others to help illuminate the nature of this perversity. So, different schools of psychological, psychoanalytic or social thought may be relevant at different times.

The seven deadly sins named in medieval times are: Pride, Lust, Wrath, Gluttony, Avarice, Envy and Sloth. As I began to look at perverse process in organisations, I began to see how many of these emotions underpinned the group dynamics that I could discern. The deadly human sins seemed to lie at the basis of perverse organisational behaviour. At first I was attracted to research the idea of pride. While a healthy degree of pride is important for growth and progress, and while company pride is a great sustaining source of encouragement for individuals to work in collective endeavours, it seemed to me that many organisations attempt to instil a false sense of pride in their members, spreading the propaganda of the latest "vision" statement to the internal market of employees as much as to their customer markets. This is reminiscent of the patriotism that political leaders wish to instil in citizens during war time. Perhaps corporate pride is the new form of patriotism—where the multinationals may be likened to countries or political entities in themselves. Certainly corporate competition has been likened to war[12] and demonstrates many of its social characteristics including the use of spies and a ruthless attitude towards the "other" as enemy. In my research I was led to Wall Street and the merchant bankers who, through to the present day, have been making countless millions from clever ways to work the money markets. In this world the competition is fierce and the stakes high. In exploring this mainly male culture, I discovered a different kind of pride. It was not the steady pride in craftsmanship of a large body of workers, but a heady, excited phallic pride that lifted the players into a willful blindness. I examine this in Chapter 3, where the case study of LTCM is presented.

That case study leads me to examine the close connection of pride and greed. Greed is a complex notion and can be directly linked to the medieval deadly sins of avarice and gluttony. In twenty-first-century corporate life, the idea of avarice and love of money is also associated with a greed for power: to be in that place that leads to gaining mass recognition, and the lifestyle of the rich and famous; the perverse culture of celebrity. I have examined this in Chapter 4 under the general heading of greed. The case of Parmalat, with its "greedy CEO" helps me to illustrate the idea of corporate greed and its perverse aspects.

In Chapter 5, I turn to examine the functioning of envy and the social defences against envy. Incorporated professional associations have a different structure to for-profit corporations. Rather than having the accountability hierarchy of organisations with vertical authority they are purportedly groups of equals with leaders voted into office.[13] A kind of horizontal authority structure operates. In such organisations envy and sibling rivalry have to be managed by other than a surrogate parental authority. Associations may be studied to throw light on the process of envy. Moreover, many corporations in post-modern times strive to create more democratic structures and practices such as found in distributed leadership, flattened hierarchy, team-based and network structures. Although these are still, at base, accountability hierarchies—there are always the boss and the owners or shareholders at the apex—and although this is not done for the sake of democracy but for increased productivity, at times they take on some of the character of associations.

An association and an accountability hierarchy meet in the company board. Chapter 6 explores the perverse dynamics found in corporate governance when directors fail to take up their role. This might be regarded as a modern form of sloth—a kind of corporate laziness or moral lassitude where the governance role is neglected. The cases of HIH Insurance and Ansett Airlines are taken as part of this exploration.

Chapter 7 examines perverse hatred and wrath as these get expressed in institutionalised bullying and abuse. Military training exemplifies the dynamics involved, although these dynamics are applicable to an analysis of bullying in corporate workplaces. While uncovering perverse dynamics through the device of looking at corporate sins, I do not attempt to make a full match with their medieval counterparts. In examining greed I focus on avarice at the expense of gluttony; I leave out lust in its direct sexual manifestation and rather put forward the idea of a lust for power. One should consider, however, that in psychoanalytic theory, sexual desire is fundamental to all desire.

It must be remembered that the emphasis here is on perversity displayed by the organisation as such, rather than simply by its leaders, or other members, even though they may embody and manifest perverse primary symptoms to the extent that they at times engage in criminal behaviours. What is explored is a group and organisation dynamic. Although it can be argued that those with power are exposed more fully to the temptations offered by the culture and hence more likely to take up such temptations, the situation is more complex. Within the perverse structure some roles are required to take up corrupt positions. They become part and parcel of the way things work. The person may condemn certain practices, but the role requires them. Tensions between person *and* role may mean that the person *in* role acts as they would not while in other roles. Such tensions may lead to the dynamics of perversity, especially the basic dynamics of splitting (the role from the person) and denial (of human responsibilities in the role) or turning a blind eye.

The Nature of System and Role

The point about the organisation dynamics cannot be overstressed. Chapter 2 describes the nature of perversity and its organisational form. In that discussion the idea of a system is assumed. By looking at organisations in terms of the decisions and agreements made within them, we begin to orientate our focus to the *system* level. Rather than seeing the organisation as a collection of individuals, each making independent decisions, we can see the organisation as a thing in its own right that gives rise to interdependent decisions.

The various systems that make up the organisation have their own structures and processes that shape the experiences of those individuals who take up the roles available and possible within these systems. I say "systems" because these include such systems as, for example, the task systems (the division of tasks into specific jobs taken on by particular work roles); political systems (the distribution of informal power between people together with its authorised distribution between work roles); and, emotional systems (the unconscious distribution of emotional experience at work, partially reliant on dispositions in the person to respond to different group pressures and task characteristics). Individuals are offered, and take up different roles in all these systems. The roles they take together form the system as a whole.[14] Each of the roles represents something of the whole and cannot be seen to operate in isolation. In addition, an organisational system in its established form validates or invalidates the experience of members and hence gives or denies access to new forms of thinking. Importantly, each role represents something of the system-as-a-whole. If you can't have a mother without a baby,[15] in the case described below, in a modern oncology unit, you can't have a surgeon without a medical oncologist or a radiologist. The role of each is created and regulated by the other.

A Case—the Agreement about Certainty

This case is given to illustrate the systems psychodynamics that operate at an organisational rather than an individual level, and provides this perspective as background to the analysis of later organisational cases. It illustrates how perverse power dynamics might begin to enter even the most altruistic of social systems, how task systems might be diverted from their avowed purpose and how denial and negation operate. It shows how primitive and pervasive is the collective human need for certainty in the face of threats to survival, how this need for certainty gathers people together as accomplices and shapes what humans can collectively tolerate.

In an action research project located in a large hospital/health system, the focus was on looking at how clinicians, mainly specialist doctors might better incorporate evidence-based medicine into their practice. My colleague[16] and I were asked to join the project through conducting a work culture analysis. Although the government funders strongly believed that finding improved ways to incorporate evidence into clinical practice should be the primary outcome of the project, there were some questions in the minds of the hospital-based project leaders about how this might be done. The project became focused in oncology.

The work led us into a series of meetings, observations and interviews with clinicians. Quite predictably we found a pattern of sub-cultures among the specialists involved. In particular, in the work sub-cultures of medical oncologists, radio-oncologists, specialist GPs and surgeons we found quite different systems of authority, epistemologies (ways of knowing) and ontologies (beliefs about the nature of things). For example, the medical oncologists had, themselves, sub-systems of those who predominantly took up clinical roles and those who took on more scientific work in clinical trials and who diligently kept abreast of the latest publications, so much so that anything published a month previously became "old" news. For these specialists the culture involved learning through peer reviewed research.

In contrast, the surgeons learned mainly in a system of authority from older, more experienced surgeons. Clinical trials in surgery cannot be achieved in the same way as those trials that test new drugs or new drug mixes and concentrations. You can trial many drugs, but you can't cut people up in a variety of different ways to see the outcome.

These sub-culture differences were interesting in themselves. However, as we proceeded through the interview process we increasingly came across reference to the idea of "the surgical personality". Admittedly a stereotype, it had some validity and was certainly an idea that prompted behaviour. In the general hospital culture, surgeons were seen as aloof, arrogant, rather rigid in their thinking and less open to change than those in other specialties. This was not simply alluded to by other clinicians, but also by some of the surgeons themselves. And, they held a great deal of authority and power. Why was this so?

As we explored the work processes within the system, we discovered that the surgeons often held the gateway to the whole referral system between the different cancer specialists. This was because a patient was highly likely to first be referred to a surgeon prior to any diagnosis of cancer. We had then, an organisational structural view on how it might be that the surgeons held power. They were gatekeepers to the other doctors' livelihoods.

But this structural analysis didn't seem enough. As we interviewed further we learned a lot more about the disputes and ambivalences among and between oncologists and other cancer clinicians. These seemed to surround the debate about how extensive should be the encouragement of chemo or radio therapy interventions in a patient with serious tumours. Trials showed that a large number of interventions did not always provide better treatment than a specific limited number. But, as one interviewee put it to me, "if it was your mother wouldn't you try just one more drug?" The anxiety that seemed to pervade the workplace often centred around, on the one hand, the fight with the disease and on the other hand the care for the patient, their quality of life and their suffering. These clinicians had no definite answers. The evidence of the so-called "gold standard" treatments could be challenged on many fronts.

This became clear in interviews as we learned of the many reasons why gold standards could not always be met in treating many actual clinical presentations, because of the patients' other life choices, or because the literature could be interpreted differentially. Often the research data could not be definitive. But, the ambivalence in the work culture became even clearer during a break in the formal interviewing process. At one time we encountered many clinicians in the airport lounge after a national meeting of the broader project. In this more relaxed setting, stories of the clinicians' own experiences of being patients emerged. The professional stance given us from the role of clinician in the formal interviews changed to a more personal stance from the role of patient. Different experiences and feelings were explored in the same people.

It gradually dawned on me that in their fear and uncertainty, members of this system needed someone who might "know" or have an answer. Or, at least this need would emerge in the basic assumption life of the system. There was a basic emotional need for certainty in the face of life and death decisions, even though conscious belief and training indicated that no such certainty existed. The surgeons filled this role of "the one who knows" and there were enormous unconscious pressures for them to stay in it. It seemed the whole system colluded in an agreement that the surgeons would take this role even though there was also consciously expressed resentment that they did so. The tension produced with the existence of unconscious pressures to assume a consciously resented and unwanted role, is one that resonates through the dynamics of many organisations and its understanding will be important throughout this book. In the case at hand, the role expressed in the "surgical personality" pervaded relations between the sub-systems of clinicians and it pervaded their training methods and referral systems. Was it not a paradox that the sub-group least dependent on an experimental or clinical trial evidence base held an important structural and emotional role in the oncology treatment system? Was "certainty" held in a place away from science, more akin to faith?

In this case, it might be argued that the medical system unconsciously created a power and authority system where the surgeons held sway and developed a collective "surgical person-ality". The system was created through the wish that someone might "know" the answers to the unanswerable questions around life and death. The people in the system both *knew* and *did not know* that no one could hold such knowledge. It was an unconscious workable perversity based on a collusive denial or turning of the blind eye, that allowed a particular authority structure to hold sway. Although in this case such a perverse stance holds the system together and allays anxieties—that is, it works as a credible defence most of the time—it may at times mean that some of the players become blind to alternate possibilities for the treatment system.

In the cases that are presented in this book, the perverse dynamics only hinted at here are made explicit in the roles of the players—usually senior personnel. But, it is the underlying societal pattern that is of major concern—the roles point us towards their underlying causes.

Notes

1. Lasch, C. (1979). *The Culture of Narcissism: American life in an age of diminishing expectations.* NY: Norton.
2. Some parts of this and the following chapter were first published in another form as: Long, S. (2002). "Destructivity and the Perverse State-of-Mind", *Organizational and Social Dynamics*, 2 (2): 179–207.
3. Hoggett, P. (1992). *Partisans in an Uncertain World: The psychoanalysis of engagement.* London: Free Association Books; Steiner, J. (1993). *Psychic Retreats: Pathological organizations in psychotic, neurotic and borderline patients.* New Library of Psychoanalysis, edited by Elizabeth Bott Spillius. London: Routledge in association with the Institute of Psychoanalysis; and Leon Gettler (2005). *Organisations Behaving Badly: A Greek tragedy of corporate pathology.* Queensland: Wiley, all refer to this phenomenon.
4. Levine, D. (2005). "The Corrupt Organization", *Human Relations* 58 (6). The quotation is from the abstract, p. 17.
5. Deal, T.E. and Kennedy, A.A. (1982). *Corporate Cultures: The rules and rituals of corporate life.* Harmondsworth: Penguin Books.
6. Bakan, J. (2004). *The Corporation: The pathological pursuit of profit and power.* London: Constable.
7. Ibid., p. 16
8. Ibid., pp. 1–2.
9. There are exceptions. James Collins and Jerry Porras examine several visionary companies arguing that many genuinely develop core ideologies beyond a simple profit motive (Collins, J.C. and Porras, J.I. (1994). *Built to Last: Successful habits of visionary companies.* NY HarperCollins). Beyond cultures that say they "put people and customers first" (a currently politically correct corporate position) some corporations manage to constructively support wider social or environmental projects, cutting into profits. Motivation for this is most likely mixed and includes the wish to improve public relations in aid of further increasing profits, but the wish to support social or environmental causes per se cannot be discounted. The point to be made here is that the corporate form within capitalism primarily promotes profit making. Philanthropy is more a motive of individuals or community groupings (namely, "community" within the organisation) despite that form.

10. Ibid., pp. 161–64.
11. "Systems Psychodynamics" is a term given to a theoretical approach that applies psychoanalytic ideas to broad systems such as organisations and society. Gould, Stapley and Stein (2004b) provide a good perspective on this approach. It was first developed at the Tavistock Institute in London in the mid-twentieth century. The term socio-analysis was coined by some working in this tradition in Australia (Bain, A. "On Socio-analysis". *Socio-Analysis*, 1 (1): 1–21)
12. Sievers, B. (2000). "Competition as War: Towards a socio-analysis of war in and among corporations". *Socio-Analysis*, 2 (2): 1–27.
13. Eliot Jaques makes the distinction between accountability hierarchies and associations. These have different forms of authority. Jaques, E. (1989). *Requisite Organization: The CEO's guide to creative structure and leadership*. USA: Carson Hall and Co.
14. Newton, J., Long, S. and Sievers, B. (eds) (2006). *Coaching in Depth: The organisational role analysis approach*. London: Karnac.
15. The British psychoanalyst Donald Winnicott is famous for this phrase, pointing out that the role of mother occurs because of the mother–baby relation. It cannot be a role outside of relation. Winnicott, D.W. (1958). *Collected Papers: Through paediatrics to psychoanalysis*. London: Tavistock Publications.
16. John Newton.

CHAPTER TWO

Understanding the Perverse State of Mind

There are five points that will be consistently emphasised throughout this book. They are the basic indicators of a perverse state of mind.[1] Derived from a study of perversion in individuals, they will first be explored in terms of individuals, later to be extrapolated to a social level of analysis.

The five indicators are first listed in their bare essentials.[2]

1. The perverse state of mind is not simply a deviation from normative morality. It has to do with individual pleasure at the expense of a more general good, often to the extent of not recognising the existence of others or their rights. It reflects a state of primary narcissism.[3]

2. The perverse state of mind acknowledges reality, but at the same time, denies it. This leads to a state of fixed ideation and fantasy to protect against the pain of seeing and not seeing at the same time.

3. The perverse state of mind engages others as accomplices in the perversion.

4. The perverse state of mind may flourish where instrumental relations have dominance in the society. This is because instrumentality ignores the rights of others to have an independent existence. This in itself is abusive. The perverse state of mind turns a blind eye.

5. Perversion begets perversion. Abusive cycles are hard to break. Corruption breeds corruption because of the complicity

of the accomplices and their subsequent denial and self-deception.

Perversion in Individual Psychology

The established dynamics of perversion at an individual system level are explored in order to evaluate the relevance of perverse dynamics at a broader systemic level. Many of the points and issues raised in this examination will be extended in later parts of the book when the idea of perversion is applied to social and organisational dynamics. The discussion here will necessarily be somewhat technical in terms of clinical psychoanalytic descriptions. What I want to do is to give you, the reader, a sense of the clinical picture and its essential characteristics. This will give insight into the perverse state of mind of individuals, and into some of the issues that concern those who study perversity. To study the organisation "as if" it had a mind, we can start to think about how a perverse state of mind might appear and operate.

The popular definition of perversity does not make as close a link to sexuality as do psychoanalytic definitions, but gives some insight into the state of mind considered by psychoanalysis. If we turn to the dictionary, perverse is noted as "persistent in error; different from what is reasonable or required; wayward; peevish; perverted; wicked; against the weight of evidence".[4] The perverse position is one of denial of reality (that is, against the weight of evidence), but denial of a reality that has been and continues to be encountered. That is, the perverse position is "persistent in its error".

So, let me examine our five points.

1. Individual Pleasure at the Expense of Others

First is the idea that perversion is not just a deviation from normality,[5] but is about individual pleasure at the expense of others. I'll try to trace some of the thinking about perversion from its classical roots. In Freudian psychoanalysis, perversion in the individual is dynamically understood as a deviation in the sexual instinct from the normal aim of adult sexuality. Perverse forms of sexuality are understood as fixations at primitive stages of development[6] often together with the disengagement of the aggressive from the libidinal instincts so that the normal balance is disturbed. Prime examples are fetishism, sadomasochism, bestiality and pederasty. The sexual impulse is on the whole evident. The sexual object is inappropriate. The aim of adult mutuality is not present.[7]

This view stems from the Freudian thesis of polymorphous perverse infantile sexuality[8] that persists unchecked into adulthood. In this, there are similarities with narcissism, especially primary narcissism. A sense of being sufficient unto oneself is present. That is, all gratification comes from oneself. Others are incidental. In secondary narcissism (the type most popularly identified) the ego is loved "as an other". That is, the psyche has achieved a distinction between self and other (i.e., has acknowledged the social realm), although this distinction is turned onto the ego as self-love. Narcissus thought he saw an "other" beautiful youth. His tragedy was that he did not know it was himself.

In perversion the ego is split. This is an outcome of the psychic defence to be explained later. It is not an entity with even the pretence of unity. It is not loved as an "other" as in secondary narcissism. It is not loved as a whole. In this sense, there is no self-love, but only the seeking of satisfaction. The situation is akin to primary narcissism—a position of self-sufficiency, where (at least in the perverse and fixed "scenario")[9] other goes unrecognised except as an extension of self.[10] Others become used and abused or taken as accomplices. Sublimation, that is, the capacity to transform egoistic pursuits into socio-centric endeavours, is not present. Perhaps it is not possible without repression. It is worth noting here that most writers who adopt the idea of a narcissistic society following Lasch tend to describe secondary rather than primary narcissism.[11]

Modern terminology names the sexual perversions as "paraphilias" marked by "rigidity of the perverse pattern, the development of an idiosyncratic 'scenario' linked to the particular perversion, and a remarkable inhibition of sexual fantasy and exploration outside the realm of this scenario".[12] The persistent clinging to the chosen scenario is as much a defence against the anxieties associated with alternative fantasies as it is to the gaining of satisfaction. It also keeps the person fixed on a familiar pattern so that movement outward into new situations is avoided.

The characteristic of individual pleasure at the expense of others might be named as selfishness in everyday language, except that in the pathological state of perversion, self is not always present in the usual sense where self and other are understood as connected but opposing terms. The selfishness of the perverse position recognises others not so much as other selves, but as objects to be used. But, even this description is not fully correct, because the relation to others is more complex. The perverse position requires that others are objects yet, at the same time, it requires them to be subjects able to experience joy and to suffer. This seeming paradox will be visited later in this book. It involves acceptance and denial of the subjectivity of the other and is linked to the next characteristic of perversity.

2. Acceptance and Denial of Reality

The perverse state of mind acknowledges reality, but also denies it. Reality threatens self-interest or previous certainty. This may be a special case of the "both/and" position. It promises the creativity of holding opposites in mind, but their connection is illusory. It offers also the destructivity of denying truth/reality and instituting parasitic relations with others.[13] This is the lure of the perverse.

Freud analysed this dynamic as achieved through splitting the ego so that both "a" and "not a" are believed.[14] In analysis this may manifest as the appearance of a "reality" side and a perverse side to the personality.[15] That is, one side of the personality can see things for what they are and as others see them, but another side of the personality is locked in a delusion. This splitting into two parts that seem to exist independently of one another is a defence against fully accepting the reality. The deluded denying side can always claim its hold when reality is unacceptable. But also, the reality being avoided is felt to be complex and confusing. In particular, it challenges the person's accepted sense of reality and threatens them with the possibility that they initially had things wrong. Behind the splitting of the ego is the fear of being in a state of uncertainty and "not knowing".

This dynamic can be seen in Freud's original analysis of fetishism.[16] This analysis is generally regarded as prototypical of the perverse dynamic in general. Following descriptions of children's theories about sexuality,[17] Freud regards the fetish as a substitute for the mother's (missing) penis—something the child believes in and despite the evidence of his senses refuses to give up. Disbelief would mean the child was wrong in his (original) desired belief that mother really did have a penis. Freud sees the strength of this belief as due to the child's narcissistic attachment to his own penis. If the child was to accept beings without penises, the possibility that he might be deprived of *his* would come into being. Better then for our potential fetishist to stay with his previous misguided sense of reality than to accept this frightening possibility. Although this seems to pertain to the male child in this theory, Freud argues that the female child also retains a belief in the female penis and the possibility of castration, and comes to believe that she has been castrated.[18] The explanation of the origin of the sexual fetish is then:

- denial of the possibility of reality (mother not having a penis), and
- retention of the fantasy of the mother with a penis (the phallic mother) and,
- replacement of the phallus with the fetish.

Freud argues that the often encountered shoe fetishist is a result of the child's gaze dropping from the awful sight of the mother's penis-less genitals, to her feet.

Important for the argument here is a denial of the position of "not knowing". The fetishist refuses the truth of sexual differentiation (which would imply the possibility of castration, given the infantile theory of one sex) and hence refuses the implication that his or her early childish theory of sexuality (i.e., where both mother and father had a penis—a sign also of power) was wrong. This would imply that he/she in fact at one stage did *not know* (the truth of sexuality— at least as espoused by adults). This seems intolerable and the child narcissistically clings to an incorrect knowledge in the face of an unwanted truth. Driven by narcissism, knowledge remains the slave of desire rather than the companion of reality.

Cognitively, it is as if the child, and later the adult, will not recognise or admit having been once in a state of ignorance or "not knowing", with its sense of powerlessness and immaturity. Moreover, a continuing anxiety persists because a continuing sense of powerlessness might result with the possible reoccurrence of such a state of not knowing. The fear of not knowing drives the subject into a conscious perverse and rigid certitude. The state of not knowing becomes feared and hated. The fear is not simply that others might think s/he is ignorant—but that one might really be ignorant and powerless. A sense of powerlessness is overdetermined. It comes from the fear of castration, the fear of not knowing and the general feelings of powerlessness present at times in the young child. The perversion thus becomes both a defence against these feelings and a source of satisfaction that heralds a triumph over powerlessness. Taken into adulthood, these feelings continue to be a powerful psychic defence.

3. The Engagement of the Accomplice

Certainty requires confirmation by another, so an accomplice is required or created. The perverse state of mind engages others as accomplices—conscious or unconscious—in the perversion. The accomplice is treated as an (autistic) extension of self. This accomplice may be woven into the perversion—a sadist needs a victim, for example. In incest, the denied, disguised or suppressed knowledge of the other (non-incestuous) parent may be an important part of the family dynamic. In the family triad, the incestuous parent attempts to engage the child and other parent as both victim and accomplice at different times (perhaps two sides of their own split ego). I have said that the perverse state of mind fails to distinguish others apart from extensions of the self. However, this does not mean that others are not a means of fascination. The objectification and humiliation of the other in many perversions aims to create an abused and used subjectivity, not a simple instrument.[19] In sadism, voyeurism and exhibitionism, the perverse subject feels excluded from the sexuality and subjectivity of the other and, in having no access, wishes to transform the situation and make the other suffer. It can be argued that the perverse state of mind, being of a split ego paradoxically experiences the other as both object and subject simultaneously. This is the position of the other as extension of a (split) self. Such a view helps in understanding the philosopher Hegel's master/slave dynamic to be discussed in a later chapter.[20]

The abuse of others is the essence of parasitical forms of relatedness and is derived from an internal perverse psychic organisation. In this split internal world in certain pathological conditions, some parts of the personality gain power over weaker parts of the personality.[21] This is no passive process, but an active collusion between different parts of the split and divided self.

> I will try to show that a perverse relationship exists and that the so called "healthy but weak" part of the self colludes and knowingly allows itself to be taken over by the narcissistic gang. Perverse relationships between members of the organisation bind them to one another and often to a leader, in ways that ensure loyalty. These very same perverse links enmesh and imprison the dependant parts of the self which cannot remain outside the organisation even when there is a disapproval of its methods and discomfort about benefiting from its advantages.[22]

This process is involved in what Steiner describes as a psychic retreat from reality. I here anticipate the way that such a process may occur in the internal life of organisations. The internal "mafia-like gang" represents a state of mind between accomplices in perverse organisational practices.

4. Instrumental Relations in Society

At a social systems level, the perverse state of mind may flourish where instrumental relations have dominance in the society. This is because instrumentality ignores the more extreme issue of abuse. We can make use of others in a non-perverse way if we recognise their rights and interests and a fair exchange is made for their being of use. This is the basic formula for the engagement of labour. Use and abuse become merged, however, in the paradox of object-subject as extension of self. The perverse state of mind is a societal state of mind that turns a blind eye to abuse. The system both knows and does not know.

Relations between people range from mutual recognition and respect through disregard to abuse. Mutual recognition and respect indicate a mature society where differences are welcomed. The perverse state of mind, by comparison, is aimed at destroying social differentiation and creating a defensive world of illusion. On the one hand, fair exchange rests on understanding and accounting for differences between people. Each person retains their individuality and may exchange what they have to offer for a different thing offered by someone else. Perverted solutions, on the other hand, triumph over the destruction of barriers, boundaries and differences.[23] Moreover, because repression is not a major defence, fantasy, at least in a restricted sense surrounding the chosen scenario, is more directly available to consciousness. The perverse state of mind collapses social and generational boundaries.[24] All become equivalent within the frame of the delusion.

This issue leads to a consideration as to whether it might not be a good thing for boundaries to be destroyed. In order for a personality or society to develop, old ways must be changed. Might the perverse position be creative as well as destructive, corrupt and criminal?

> On the one hand, there is the tendency to see perversion as a transgressive, disruptive, dangerous force, a metonymy for the human desire and capacity to break down the social hierarchy and overturn meanings ... the little boy denying his mother's "castration" is a creative rebel for whom the established order of things is not sufficient ... On the other hand there is the tendency to see perversion as conservative, rigid and fixated, a mentality or practice ... concerned with endless unchanging repetition of a "script" carefully constructed in advance.[25]

This debate is relevant to issues of entrepreneurship in industry. It becomes centred on whether or not some perverse-like dynamics are necessarily corrupt and linked to human destructivity. Do we have room for corporate cowboys who through their creativity bring new ventures into being yet, later, make mistakes, especially in their risk-taking and step over the line, particularly in the cover-up of their mistakes?[26]

There are sadistic elements in the infant and child. While these may be related to adult criminality, the evidence is usually retrospective from case studies and can say little about the general connection. Most of the usual childhood sadistic impulses become tempered and socialised through the child's growing experience of how to control them and behave decently. Even though some psychoanalysts regard "perversions as manifestations of the death instinct—impulses that distort sexuality",[27] other analysts find in perversion a seed of healthy desire.

The very word perversion means that there is something which has become perverted. We presume that this something is real and also good. "Perverted" suggests that it is damaging in some way to the development of the personality and the individual's creative capacity.[28]

Drawing from clinical examples and literary works, especially the work of de Sade, Janine Chasseguet-Smirgel claims that the perverse solution to the problem of an unwanted reality involves regression to the anal-sadistic phase.[29] This is because the unwanted reality (the possibility of castration and the inability to possess mother at the oedipal stage) implies recognition of the child's sexual immaturity and inability to fulfil the desire of the mother. Agreeing with the idea that denial alongside acknowledgement is a major defence, she analyses the perversion in terms of its creativity and destructivity. "My hypothesis", she says, "is that perversion represents a reconstitution of chaos, out of which there arises a new kind of reality, that of the anal universe. This will take the place of the psycho-sexual genital dimension, that of the father".[30] This also provides for a kind of creativity of a perverse universe, albeit one which is a sham or a semblance.

One is reminded of Freud's analysis of Judge Schreber whose "end-of-the-world" fantasy gives rise to a reconstructed universe. The difference from the psychotic reconstruction is that in perversion the reconstitution is specifically in the form of idealised anality, because the world of the (genital) father is not reached in development. This is linked to mass group psychology where the superego (conscience derived from the parental authority) often fails as the members become their own ideal and follow an ideology without question. The führer is not a real father but a figure of mass identification. Following Freud's ideas on group psychology, Chasseguet-Smirgel attempts, as have many, to understand why ordinary people at times give up their own powers of judgement to join with a group ideology that renders everyone (of the in-group) as uniform, and the out-group as dispensable. She regards this as a perverse process. This idea will be pursued more fully in Chapter 5.

For present purposes, Chasseguet-Smirgel's argument has particular relevance for two reasons. First, she considers how perversion works within a cycle of destructivity and creativity and that central to this is a challenge to the laws of nature and of society—all boundaries must be broken by the perverse, including generational boundaries. This argument has echoes of the current insistence on the promotion of youth and dismissal of age in some organisations. Second, she considers this within a social context, noting how the destruction of social orders is linked to public expressions of the perverse. She says,

> shouldn't we associate historical ruptures which give an inkling of the advent of a new world, with the confusion between sexes and generations, peculiar to perversions, as if the hope for a new social and political reality went hand in hand with an attempt at destroying sexual reality and truth?[31]

In a similar vein Phillip Rieff says,

> At the breaking point a culture can no longer maintain itself as an established span of moral demands. Its jurisdiction contracts; it demands less, permits more. Bread and circuses become confused with right and duty. Spectacle becomes a functional substitute for sacrament. Massive regressions occur with large sections of the population returning to levels of destructive aggression historically accessible to it.[32]

The individual psychic defence of denial and the wish for certitude seem basic to the abolition of boundaries. The perverse state of mind is not lost in uncertainty because nothing really matters and anything goes. Chasseguet-Smirgel and Rieff see the part played by this position in cataclysmic-type social change processes, even if they also see the personal destructivity implied. The "established span of moral demands" noted by Rieff is challenged and attacked unconsciously in perversion and consciously in corruption where individual forms of morality overtake culturally established norms.[33]

5. Perversion Begets Perversion

Abusive cycles are hard to break. Corruption breeds corruption because of the complicity of the accomplices and their subsequent denial and self-deception. The difficulties in rehabilitating child abusers is well know. To better understand the tenacious and persistent hold of perversion on the mind, it can be distinguished from the mental illnesses of neurosis and psychosis.

Psychoanalysis has explored the ways mind is related to pleasure and to reality (the two mental principles).[34] The neurotic/normal position primarily employs repression, that is, active forgetting and removal from conscious thought. Reality becomes distorted because parts of it are unbearable. But repressed thoughts return and when they threaten to become conscious, defensive mechanisms are employed. These act to distort reality. For Freud, the neurotic position results from the oedipal conflict and its resolution at least in the recognition of the incest taboo, the threat of castration and the need to find one's own love objects outside the family. The relation to reality is adjustive and when the neurotic achieves normality (that is, when the neurotic is more able to think his or her thoughts rather than turn unwanted thoughts into symbolic symptoms) then the relation to reality can be based non-defensively on experience.

The psychotic position involves a severe splitting of both reality and the ego because much of reality is hated and rejected. Attention and focus turn inward and thinking is out of touch with reality and dominated by fantasy. In this position destructivity is aimed at the relation with reality and hence thinking and linking are destroyed because thinking is a transformation of experience within a real but frustrating environment.[35] The psychotic position is narcissistic and the relatedness to others is detached and split off.

How then can we define the perverse? As with the psychotic position, the ego is split. However, the relation to reality is more ambivalent. As with repression, the major neurotic defence, denial implies some acceptance of reality prior to its rejection. However, unlike repression, in denial recognition of reality sits ambiguously side by side with its denial, even in conscious fantasy. This describes a certain psychological position or state of mind; the purely perverse, if you like.[36]

In attempting a definition, it is not easy to locate the perverse as a mental illness in the same way as the neuroses and psychoses. Although the psychosocial ideas of developmental arrest and psychoneurotic defence are seen as central to most theories, so too are the socio-legal ideas of corruption, aggression and illegality in terms of social boundaries. This difficulty of definition shows itself most strongly in the way that societies handle perversity. The defining line tends to stand more with the law than through ideas of intrinsic health or illness. Whereas the anxious neurotic and deluded psychotic are accepted as ill, debates still rage about the aetiology and treatment of sex offenders, for instance. Although modern psychiatry locates perversion within the character disorders or as symptoms of psychosis, a clear distinctive definition is unavailable.[37] It is sufficient to say here that if we are to understand the perverse state of mind within the social system (rather than as individually characterological), its essential system dynamics as outlined here are more pertinent than its place in current popular or psychiatric classifications of individuals.

One other factor in the psychoanalytic understanding of perversion is raised when we consider the relation between perversion and dissociation. The perverse is sometimes understood as the opposite of neurosis insofar as fantasy is not repressed but overt and the major defences are denial and displacement. However, denial is also employed in dissociative states, normally considered as neurotic, such as amnesia, fugue and multiple personality.

Dissociative states are quite different from anxiety states (which are the very essence of neurosis) and they seem to require a relation to reality similar to that described in perversion. Take the extreme case of multiple personality. Here the ego is split, the subject both "knows" and does "not know" the different personalities internally present, an illusory reality is created and whole social contexts or created lives are unconsciously drawn on as "accomplices". A key feature is the presence of a manufactured identity. Research tends to show that dissociation is a response to trauma, psychological or physical. It is present, for example, in post-traumatic stress syndrome. In particular cases the dissociation may be a delayed response to early childhood trauma. The dynamic involves a desire to quite literally get out of a painful body or psyche and is thus a more radical form of defence than repression. When it is a particular *state of knowing* that is rejected (i.e., a painful set of thoughts), then the perverse structure of dissociative states becomes clearer. This so often constitutes the dissociative response of the abused child. It is not simply the trauma and pain that are rejected, but also the knowledge of the abuse and, perhaps, of an abuser who is also a major figure for dependency.

This discussion is important because it provides a clue to the links between perverse denial, dissociative states and illusory identity. One solution of the victim of sadistic or sexual abuse is to become the accomplice or even to replicate the abuse later in life through identification with the aggressor. This is one way in which abuse is perpetuated. Although abuser, victim and accomplice are quite different roles with different emergent behavioural symptoms, they are each caught within a parasitic and perverse system, whether or not these role holders are consciously aware of this. The roles they hold demand they play out perverse scenarios in particular ways and the person *in* role may feel quite conflicted about this. This is important in the consideration of workplace bullying, for example, where the roles of bully, victim and bystander become caught in a perverse system, sometimes as a result of multiple collusions and accomplices and where the exposure of the system threatens or disturbs the ongoing power bases of many role holders. The players are not necessarily personally unconflicted in their roles, but if the bullying is part of a broader culture their disquiet may be reduced through systemically supported denial. This will be revisited in Chapter 7.

A Perverse Society

The progression from discussing individual character to discussing social dynamics cannot be made in a simple way. Here, the idea of a perverse society parallels ideas such as Christopher Lasch's idea of the narcissistic socety where a major dynamic is understood as an operating principle for society at large. There is no suggestion that every, or even the majority of individuals personally demonstrates the dynamic in its clinical sense. What is suggested is that the society operates systemically on the basis of the identified dynamic and that this in turn will affect the individuals and shape their behaviours.

I have been discussing the perverse state of mind in terms of the individual. But, states of mind cannot be adequately conceptualised in terms of the isolated individual. Essentially, a "state of mind" whilst evidenced in individuals and enacted by them, is a social concept.[38] At the very least we must take account of the individual in context.

My argument here looks at the ways in which a narcissistic society promotes the development of an increasingly perverse society, or at least increases major pockets of socially enacted perversion. I will now examine the nature of narcissism in society and the workplace and then examine how perverse structures arise due to additional elements of denial, "turning a blind eye" and seeking (unconscious) accomplices in corrupt behaviour. A major distinction between the (secondary) narcissistic and the perverse states of mind must be made. This is posed theoretically around the distinction given earlier between primary and secondary narcissism. It is more practically recognised in terms of the social defence of denial, use of others as accomplices and the dissolution or flouting of social boundaries in terms of social agreements. This latter breaking of boundaries is found in corruption. The perverse is distinguished from the self-love/ self-interest of the narcissistic dynamic, which stays within the law, or at least recognises the law and attempts to stay within it. Moreover, the (secondary) narcissist craves the love and recognition of others. The perverse position uses others in a far more detached manner.

The second half of the twentieth century produced, at least in the developed countries, an increasingly narcissistic or egotistical society.[39] High levels of consumerism and withdrawal into a "me first" position are seen to have permeated group and organisational life. At an institutional level, accountability to the community by corporate or private owners of public services and utilities has declined, and globalised markets that serve a privileged population while disadvantaging others who have limited or no access, have emerged.[40] Moreover, the increased privatisation of services such as transport, health and education in an increasingly service-oriented industry sector, together with an increased secularisation of society has changed the nature of large institutions. In place of a diversity of institutions we have rendered them equivalent within a corporate business and economic paradigm or discourse.[41] The heir to such a culture of narcissism may well be a perverse society. This is because cultural narcissism allows the development of a blind eye to perverse and exploitative behaviour, through increased privatisation and withdrawal of checks and balances from the public sphere.

While socially secondary narcissism indicates a withdrawal from openly collective life and thinking and turns the libidinal instincts in on the self, perversion indicates an exploitative attitude, with the other regarded primarily as *an accomplice* in the achievement of exploitation. This reveals the more autistic position of primary narcissism. The culture of private consumerism is based on instrumental relatedness. That is, a relationship where people use one another to gain their own particular ends or fulfil their own specific agendas with little attention to mutual aims or to the quality of the relationship per se. Such distanced relatedness with minimal personal investment in the relationship seems inevitably to lead to a corrupt and exploitative attitude in large sections of society. At least, it allows for corruption and exploitation to occur in the face of a withdrawn and distanced, almost negligible collective or social body. For example, the achievements of freedom of information legislation and increased consumer protection for the individual are reduced or counterbalanced by new terrorist laws that allow people to be detained without trial for extended periods of time. The fact that many developments in the biological sciences now fall under "commercial in confidence" rules means that open social debate is delayed or elided and socially authorised checks and balances are minimised. Despite the fact that social global movements are evolving, for example S11, so too is privatised and less scrutinised research. There seems to be a divide between people as citizens and people as corporate members. I will revisit this idea in Chapter 8.

There are many signs that currently the perverse is alive and well. Stories of abuse and their cover-up are constantly surfacing, whether perpetrated by individuals or more insidiously within institutions. Increasing numbers of stories of child abuse within the Church have surfaced. There is also increasing evidence of abuse within work organisations. At one level, organisation members may feel that their managers steal their ideas and that they are given no recognition for their contributions. This is now understood as abusive. Beyond this are the stories of physical and emotional abuse. For example, a kind of social voyeurism exists where all aspects of the employee's behaviour are under scrutiny—some feel, for example, that they must be "on call" even when taking sick leave. One of my clients, for example, is subject to calls from the CEO at any time of day or night and was forced at one stage to turn the mobile off and to disengage the home phone as the only way of preventing this intrusion. None of these practices may be essentially new. In fact, we might rejoice in the fact that what is new is their exposure to community concern. However, the stark contradiction between avowed social values and these practices is evident and accepted. Avowed values and practice are split apart.

At a more "normal" social level, perverse themes are publicly more acceptable. Popular films, whilst increasingly pushing the boundaries of the depiction of violence, sadism and perverse sexuality have become more directly and explicitly interested in the character of the perverse. The film "Hannibal" is one example, as is the film "Quills" which romaticises the last years of the Marquis de Sade and includes a romanticisation of such perverse activities as necrophilia. Recent heavy metal bands have included more and more perverse themes in their music around abuse, rape, suicide, sadism and masochism. This is not simply a fringe phenomenon. Marilyn Manson, a singer who includes many such themes and who, one might say perversely, takes his stage name from a combination of Marilyn Monroe and Charles Manson, has had popular top-selling CDs. Many of his songs, although forming a critique of a perverse society by demonstrating its effects, themselves come to be expressive of perverse themes.

Consider also the advent of "reality television". There has been a rise in television shows such as "Big Brother". Here, a group of people are put together and their every interaction, including quite private activities is taped and viewed by an audience called upon to judge them. Whereas the narcissistic "soaps" encouraged viewers to follow the lives of fictitious characters through their personal and interpersonal histories, viewers are now taken into the filmed personal and intimate daily lives of real families or groups. This reflects a longing on the part of the viewer to regain a lost community intimacy. However, the result is not a reconnected community but the institution of a voyeur and exhibitionist on different sides of a screen. Individualism and narcissism have led to collective perversion.

Often the description of perversion itself becomes perverse—a case of the defence joining the drive. Whether we see these popular culture phenomena as a needed exploration of previously hidden themes (sometimes even a criticism—where old boundaries are challenged and discarded), or as perverse expressions in themselves, does not detract from noting the rise of public interest in perversion.

Narcissism in the Workplace

The post-war baby boom generation has been increasingly popularly described as narcissistic. This characterisation is dominated by reference to individualism, the private regulation of family life and the rise of consumerism. The field of psychoanalytic approaches to organisations has well documented the culture of narcissism within work, management and organisational settings. In the workplace, the move from bureaucracies to conglomerates of business units, and the privatisation of large institutions has structurally institutionalised narcissism. This is evident also in changed employment patterns from tenured to contract positions with an increase in casual labour even in non-seasonal industries; and in changed workplace attitudes where self-promotion is encouraged above extended company loyalty. The newly described fifth basic assumption Me[42] is seen to dominate in networked or loosely coupled forms of organisation. These tend to encourage self-authorisation, where recourse to the group is deemed an unnecessary delay and personal triumphs are the main way forward when climbing the career ladder.

An Attitude of Acquisition, Exploitation and Narcissism

A form of organisation increasingly favoured in the global economy requires loosely coupled semi-autonomous business units themselves broadly accountable to large multinational conglomerates. These units are understood to be flexible and mobile, able to make decisions quickly and decisively and hence be both producers and consumers within a broader organisational network. In many ways, it is as if late twentieth-century organisations had finally caught up (structurally and dynamically) with the changes that came when the extended family transformed itself into networks of nuclear families during the nineteenth century. Such changes, stimulated by new ways of connecting to the environment—especially including new technologies—bring with them new forms of creativity. They also bring new forms of destructivity based on the illusion that these units are self-sustained, narcissistically self-sufficient, and not responsible for or to the wider system of which they are a part. Here, there is not an intention simply to decry the changes, although sometimes change is not necessarily for the best. Adaptation and change are inevitable, often life sustaining, even desirable in the best sense of the word. The focus, however, will be on understanding the destructive.

The psychoanalytic study of organisations has previously considered destructivity in terms of unconscious neurotic or psychotic processes. Chapman,[43] for example, looks at the hatred of task and its resultant unconscious corruption in the tradition of social and individual defences. However, much of what we currently understand as destructive in organisational life is linked to the seemingly deliberate and callous behaviour of corporations, through their senior management, towards a workforce considered as a dispensable and exploitable resource. This exploitative attitude is most clearly seen in those stories of dismissal where the employee is given little notice but told to clear their desk and leave immediately, presumably to minimise any real or fantasised retaliatory anger by the person so treated. It is also implicit in those organisational changes where re-engineering is employed as a means of shedding personnel. Often organisational consultants are employed to expedite the process under the guise of development. There are many situations where the consultant is seemingly required to explore options while the real agenda is for them to "recommend" the restructuring solution pre-determined by the board of the organisation or their senior managers.

Of course there are times when organisational reality requires that jobs be cut. Long-term objectives and short-term survival each has its demands on company size. I am referring here not to such necessities, but to an underlying exploitative and accompanying acquisitive attitude. Such an attitude is essentially propelled by a socially structured narcissistic greed and is by no means restricted to boards and senior management. If it were, trade unionism would still be strong and the major social differentiation would still lie between the industrialists and the workers. The bigger divide nowadays is between the fully employed and those who work sessionally, seasonally or part-time. Those with superannuation provisions, for example, or an investment portfolio, or even enough regular income to pay off a mortgage are intrinsically part of the acquisitive society.

The social structure under consideration here is a combination of factors.

1. Capitalism sustained through self-regulating markets (which nonetheless exclude many from within the community and are subject to irrational forces within groups and institutions) and the strong conviction that the economy is *the* major social system.

2. An extension in the last century from commodity to money markets at a globalised level. The concept of arbitrage (making non-risk profits through taking advantage of currency, bond and interest rate differences across different economies or markets) in many cases denies the reality that in a healthy society money is generated from work: some effort and risk. This denial, taken alongside knowledge that labour outside the money market is the real basis of any economy, lies at the very heart of perverse structure as I shall go on to demonstrate in a later chapter through the case of LTCM.

3. The degradation and pollution of the environment through a vacillating denial of the destructive effects of our way of living. The breaking of environmental agreements by the US is testimony to the destructivity that the US culture is implicated in. The fact that Australia continually buys out of such agreements declares our unwillingness to let go of an attitude that denies facts and sustains a belief that "we know better". Again, I will demonstrate the relation of such attitudes to perverse structure and dynamics. The acquisitive and exploitative attitude is deeply embedded in cultural (secondary) narcissism. This invites increasingly perverse behaviour.

Perverse Organisation

Distinctions need be drawn between corruption, immorality, deviancy and perversion. First, when looking from a psychoanalytic or socio-analytic perspective the role of unconscious dynamics and structures is critical. The jury is still out, so to speak, on the aetiology of corrupt and criminal behaviour.

Second, while organisations and enterprises may contain individuals who are corrupt, immoral, deviant or perverse, the focus here is on the system beyond the individual. Just as an individual need not be seen as perverse because there are perverse elements (to every personality) so a system need not be ineffective, destructive or fail because it has some few corrupt or immoral individuals. We need to look more broadly at the system, considering whether or not it is suffering the unconscious dynamics of perversity at the system level. This requires a critical refocus.

Take the five points about the perverse state of mind presented earlier. Can they be understood in terms of the broader system's state? As a reminder, in brief they are:

1. The perverse state of mind is not simply a deviation from normative morality. It has to do with individual pleasure at the expense of a more general good. It reflects a state of primary narcissism.

2. The perverse state of mind acknowledges the reality concerned, but also denies it.

3. The perverse state of mind engages others as accomplices in the perversion.

4. The perverse state of mind may flourish where instrumental relations have dominance in the society. This is because instrumentality ignores the more extreme issue of abuse. It is a societal state of mind that turns a blind eye.

5. Perversion begets perversion. Abusive cycles are hard to break. Corruption breeds corruption because of the complicity of the accomplices and their subsequent denial and self-deception.

Consider the following organisational examples.

The practice of 12-hour shifts has increased in a variety of industries across the western industrialised countries. The production of photographic materials, policing, maintenance of aircraft and mining are a few examples. Justification for two 12-hour rather than three eight-hour shifts is basically an economic one. Workers are encouraged into this practice by promises of more leave and flexible working hours. To fulfil this, sometimes shifts are rotated so workers have both day and night shifts—sometimes in rather rapid succession. The health and safety risks in 12-hour shifts are known. The last four hours are stressful to the workers. Adjusting to night shifts takes some time. Yet the practice is on the increase, justified through seductive instrumental and economic considerations. Is this perverse, given what *is known yet denied*?

Health risks to workers in industries using asbestos were well known by senior management long before they were publicised widely, as were the health risks of cigarette smoking. At an institutional level, such risks were not unknown, they were denied, perhaps with a split in the organisations involved where the knowledge and the denial sat side by side. This is perverse. It may feel mad (read psychotic) to individuals locked into the split-off parts, but at the institutional level it seems perverse.

Increasing amounts of self-authorisation by executives in multinational companies may seem to indicate high levels of trust in these individuals. Perhaps this is largely justified. However, in some cases the lack of checking back with a group—that is, the lack of authorisation as a representative process—increases the possibility of corruption. In such cases the self-authorisation seeks an unconscious accomplice in the partner organisation that does not check the support behind the self-authorisation. The case of the 27-year-old derivatives trader, Nick Leeson, with Barings bank in the mid-1990s is one instance. Here a self-authorised individual was able to continue betting unsuccessfully on a rise in the Japanese stock market far in excess of the bank's ability to meet his costs. His capacity to meet the costs he incurred—which ran into billions of pounds, i.e., beyond the assets of the bank—was questioned by no one. One might say he perverted the task, but *the lack of checks and balances in the system* really did this. Stein[44] provides an interesting analysis focused on the bank's unconscious collusion with the trader. This was a case of individual secondary narcissism and greed, but also a case of institutional perversion.

The recent multi-billion-dollar collapse of HIH Insurance in Australia (more fully discussed in Chapter 6) has revealed that its former CEO made an important decision to sell the group's retail insurance business without informing the board. The perversion of authority into personal power is an insidious organisational process. It always requires accomplices, some of whom are fearful, some of whom are greedy, and most of whom join in the denial.

An Australian company (not named because this information comes through a client) was in dire financial straits and this was not picked up by the auditors and not made known to the shareholders by (a knowing) senior management and the board. The consulting company doing the audit also provided other (more profitable) services to the company. They did this through gaining the audit work and then "cross-selling" other services. What conscious or unconscious contracting is occurring here? The case of Andersen in the recent Enron scandal comes to mind. It is as if the dependency relation set up between consultant and client promotes two relations towards this reality: one of acceptance and one of denial.

The Case of Enron

The story of Enron as it grew from a small Texas utility trading natural gas to an international company "trading almost anything that could be traded" can be read as a case of greed, corruption, deception and subterfuge amongst its senior executives. Was it an example of perversion? The analysis here can only be brief. The reader may want to pursue its implications more deeply and a readable summary of the case may be found in Fusaro and Miller,[45] while an analysis in psychoanalytic terms can also be found in Levine.[46]

First, it is clear that some of the top executives were corrupt. In particular, the practice of creating special purpose entities (SPEs) to finance Enron's deals yet keep the debts off the company's records was a tactic devised to give the appearance of profitability. This manipulated appearances and raised Enron's share price on the financial markets. The executives, of course, gained personally through trading shares. As with many companies, raising the share price became a priority. For many CEOs the market becomes a source of great anxiety.[47] At the expense of real growth, an illusion was created. Through their expertise in utilities markets, Enron staff learned to create markets with themselves as traders. They would buy gas, and later electricity, water and almost anything, through the internet and sell to distributors. Very simply, the further they got from their initial expertise, the less they understood of the markets they were creating and the more they suffered real losses, which they covered up.

The question is whether or not the illusion was believed, and by whom. People and companies who bought shares that leapt to extraordinary heights obviously believed the illusion. But they were misled. An anonymous memo to the CEO from a senior manager late in 2001, shortly before the rapid slide into bankruptcy, showed her knowledge of the situation and how it would damage shareholders, including many company employees who might also lose their jobs. Her words were later seen as suggesting a cover-up. Fusaro and Miller argue the case of greed, arrogance and aggrandisement. Some of the senior executives got out with a lot of money. But they also argue the CEO Ken Lay's adamant and rigid belief in free markets to the extent that any market whatsoever could be created. Enron's risk lay in their becoming always a "counterparty" in the markets they created. They took all the financial risks and relied on image in order to increase liquidity—their market edge.

It could be read that Lay believed his own image whilst at the same time creating the deceptions that would keep it alive. We have to ask was this outright deception or dogmatic certitude that sustained an illusion, perhaps both. One could argue that the deception and corruption was invoked to shore up the illusion. The perverse quality comes through in the denial about real profits vs. paper profits. Although debts were hidden, many must have seen through this device. But it was as if the company and its trading partners denied the need to scrutinise the accounts. (Eventually in 2001, Skilling—one of the executives who briefly took on the CEO role, resigned after failing to show true profits on demand.) It also comes through in the collusion with Andersen the auditors. They became yet another set of accomplices. The instrumental relations between these executives, the market players and the auditors, were reflected in the corporate culture, described by Fusaro and Miller as ruthless, where a "rank and yank" strategy was used to employ high achievers but deliberately factor-in removal of the so-called bottom 10 per cent every six months. This latter practice alone was self-destructive because many of those "yanked" took Enron knowledge to other rival companies.

Whereas in this case we can see the operation of narcissistic, greedy grandiose *individual players*, the organisational *system* displays itself as illusory, self-deceptive, in denial and with a sense of "other" only to be exploited. Markets are quite anonymous others, and employees were seen as exploitable commodities. The practice of rewarding senior executives with share options (commonplace in the corporate world and now recognised as perverse)[48] leads to an over-emphasis on share price rather than substantive profit. In short, the development and reward of (secondary) narcissistic characteristics led eventually to the creation of a perverse system.

Notes

1. State of mind refers to a particular co-configuration of thoughts, attitudes, perceptions, emotions and beliefs that also link to particular behavioural tendencies. A warlike state of mind, for example, indicates the co-configuration of angry and hostile thoughts and emotions together with the propensity to attack (sometimes created) enemies.

2. These ideas are drawn from general psychoanalytic theory with particular reference to: the works of Sigmund Freud; Lacan, J. (1977). *Ecrits*. London: Tavistock Publications; Nobus and Downing (eds) (2006). *Perversion: Psychoanalytic perspectives*, pp. 19–38. London: Karnac; Pajaczkowska, C. (2000). *Ideas in Psychoanalysis: Perversion*. UK: Icon Books; Steiner, J. (1993). *Psychic Retreats: Pathological organizations in psychotic, neurotic and borderline patients*. New Library of Psychoanalysis, edited by Elizabeth Bott Spillius. London: Routledge in association with the Institute of Psychoanalysis; and Chasseguet-Smirgel, J. (1984). *Creativity and Perversion*. London: Free Association Books.

3. Sigmund Freud refers to primary and secondary narcissism in his 1914 paper *On Narcissism: An introduction. SE*, XIV: 73–102, London: Hogarth Press, 1957. The distinction is critical. Narcissism basically refers to self-love as in the myth of Narcissus, the youth who fell in love with his own reflection in a pool. In primary narcissism, the individual is egocentrically focused on self with no sense that others even exist. In secondary narcissism, the individual is in love with him or herself as a social being. That is, a person who recognises others and is part of a social group. Because of this, secondary narcissism occurs when a person is in love with themselves "as if" they were another person. This is not so much an autistic preoccupation, as in primary narcissism, as a pre-occupation with a self that is a reflection of the society surrounding that self. This fits with the narcissism of someone who, for example, wishes to be adored by others and who identifies himself with heroes or celebrities who are admired.

4. Oxford English Dictionary.

5. Because the acceptance of diversity within the sexual practices of adults has differed throughout history and across cultures, what is classified as perverse obviously changes. For Sigmund Freud, homosexuality was accounted amongst the perversions. Nowadays we think differently.

6. Classical psychoanalysis considered that psychological disturbances were often due to the individual being preoccupied with unresolved problems from an earlier stage in their life.

7. This explanation should not be confused with a simple view of deviation from normative morality or of sexual exploration and diversity of expression. It is an explanation of psychic developmental arrest or fixation that may not always be easy to demonstrate outside of analysis.

8. Polymorphous infantile sexuality refers to the idea that infants, while experiencing sexual sensuality, are experiencing this in a more diffuse sense than adults. Their sexual sensations are not focused on the sexual organs but on several erogenous zones such as the mouth, the anus and the skin in general. In this view, infants can happily derive pleasurable gratification from all over.

9. The perverse "scenario" refers to the fixed fantasy required both to achieve gratification and to defend against associated anxieties. Although normal sexual practice may involve favoured or even necessary fantasies, the perverse secenario is more fixed and essential. It may be linked directly to orgasm, but gratification of perverse tendencies may not require this. An aggressive aim may alone be satisfied.

10. Sigmund Freud's "polymorphous perversity" and Wilfred Bion's idea of the parasitic relation vs. the positive K (knowledge) link are relevant here. Freud argues that sexuality begins as "polymorphous perverse" with no particular aim but its own satisfaction. See Freud, S. Three Essays on the Theory of Sexuality (1905). In: *Sigmund Freud: On Sexuality*. Harmondsworth: Penguin, 1977. Bion considers that links between thoughts (and, by extension, people) may be parasitic, where one is used by the other without any real communion or intercourse. These ideas are extended in Bion's theory of thinking developed across several years and explored in, for example, Bion, W.R. (1962). *Learning from Experience*. London: Karnac (1984); Bion, W.R. (1967). *Second Thoughts*. London: Karnac Books; Bion, W.R. (1970). *Attention and Interpretation*. London: Tavistock Publications.

11. Lasch, C. (1979). *The Culture of Narcissism: American life in an age of diminishing expectations*. NY: Norton.
12. Kernberg, O. (2006). "Perversion, perversity and normality: diagnostic and therapeutic considerations". In: D. Nobus and L. Downing (eds) (2006). *Perversion: Psychoanalytic perspectives*, pp. 19–38. London: Karnac, p. 22.
13. It should be noted that by "reality" is meant the current evolution of the knowledge of society or, in Bion's terms, the reality-oriented work group. Bion, W. (1961). *Experiences in Groups*. London: Tavistock Publications.
14. Sigmund Freud describes how the ego, when traumatised may take on a defensive mode whereby a reality is both dismissed and accepted. "On the one hand, with the help of certain mechanisms he rejects reality and refuses to accept any prohibition; on the other hand, in the same breath he recognises the danger of reality, takes over the fear of that danger as a pathological symptom and tries subsequently to divest himself of the fear." (Freud, S. (1940). "Splitting of the Ego in the Process of Defence", p. 462. In: Freud, S., *On Metapsychology and the Theory of Psychoanalysis*. Harmondsworth: Penguin Books, 1984.) This description fits the reactions of many corporate leaders *in role* in relation to some of the threats to their continued, entrenched, yet misguided, business activities, as described in various case studies in this book. I stress *in role* because I am not suggesting that these people are perverse but that the organisational practice is perverse. This will be developed as a theme in later chapters.
15. Goldberg, A. (2006). "An overview of perverse behaviour". In: D. Nobus and L. Downing (eds) (2006). *Perversion: Psychoanalytic perspectives*, pp. 39–58. London: Karnac.
16. Freud, S. (1927). "Fetishism". *SE*, 21. London: Hogarth Press, 1978.
17. Freud, S. (1905), op. cit. The child's initial theory is that there is just one sex and this sex has a penis. On encountering naked females (e.g., a sister or the mother) the childhood theory is that this person must be castrated.
18. I will hold back here from arguments and readings from a more feminist perspective and outline the argument as put forward by Freud. It rests on his outline of the sexual theories of children that are retained in the adult unconscious. It helps explore the dynamics of perversion, notwithstanding that Freud may have been mistaken in some of his theories with regard to women. The "reality" of

castration is held within the child's sexual theory that there is only one sex with two forms: with a penis or castrated.

19. Benvenuto, S. (2006). "Perversion and charity: an ethical approach". In: D. Nobus and L. Downing (eds) (2006) *Perversion: Psychoanalytic perspectives*, pp. 59–78. London: Karnac.
20. Hegel, G.W.F. (1998). *Phenomenology of Spirit*. In S. Houlgate (ed.) *The Hegel Reader*. Oxford: Blackwell Publishers.
21. Steiner, J. (1993), op. cit.
22. Ibid., p. 104.
23. Chasseguet-Smirgel, J. (1984), op. cit.
24. Ibid.
25. Downing, L. (2006). "Perversion, historicity, ethics". In: D. Nobus and L. Downing (eds) (2006). *Perversion: Psychoanalytic perspectives*, pp. 149–64. London: Karnac, pp. 153–4.
26. Trevor Sykes discusses the corporate entrepreneurs in Australia in the 1980s looking at where they had successes and where things went wrong. Sykes, T. (1994). *The Bold Riders*. St Leonards, NSW: Allen and Unwin.
27. Hinshelwood, R. (1991). *A Dictionary of Kleinian Thought*. London: Free Association Books.
28. Symington, J. and Symington, N. (1996). *The Clinical Thinking of Wilfred Bion*. London and New York: Routledge.
29. Chasseguet-Smirgel, J. (1984), op. cit.
30. Ibid., p. 11.
31. Ibid., p. 2.
32. Rieff, P. (1966). *The Triumph of the Therapeutic: Uses of faith after Freud*. Great Britain: Penguin Books, p. 200.
33. Levine, D.P. (2005). "The Corrupt Organisation". *Human Relations*, 58 (6): 723–40.
34. Sigmund Freud looked upon the neuroses and psychoses as presenting different symptoms due to their different relations to reality. Freud, S. (1924). "Loss of Reality in Neurosis and Psychosis" *SE*, XIX: 183–90. London: Hogarth Press, 1957.
35. Wilfred Bion's work on thinking and psychosis examines attacks on linking.
36. Apart from the perverse psychic position or state of mind, perverse sexuality and behaviour may be found within patients diagnosed as neurotic, psychotic, borderline or narcissistic according to modern psychoanalytic and psychiatric descriptions and classifications. See Kernberg, O. (2006), op. cit.

37. Michel Foucault has written extensively about historical changes in defining mental illness and abnormality. He emphasises the way that definitions have been torn between medicine and the law. See, for example: Foucault, M. (2003). *Abnormal: Lectures at the College de France 1974–75*. London: Verso; and Foucault, M. (1963). *Madness and Civilization: A history of insanity in the age of reason*. NY: Random House.

38. Rom Harré, a British philosopher argues that mind is a social, not an individual phenomenon. See Harré, R. (1984). "Social Elements as Mind". *British Journal of Medical Psychology*, 57: 127–35. Wilfred Bion's work on groups (Bion, W.R. (1961), op. cit.) also demonstrates the idea of mind as located in the group, while the work of Jacques Lacan (Lacan, J. (1977), op. cit.) posits the idea of the Symbolic register of experience where the person experiences the world through the lens of his or her immersion in the symbolic social field.

39. See, for example, Lasch, C. (1979), op. cit.; Miller, E. (1999). "Dependency, alienation or partnership? The changing relatedness of the individual to the enterprise". In: Robert French and Russ Vince (eds) *Group Relations Management and Organization*. Oxford: Oxford University Press; and Lawrence, W.G., Bain, A. and Gould, L. (1996). "The Fifth Basic Assumption". *Free Associations*, 6 (37): 28–55.

40. I recognise that global markets have opened up trade for many third world countries. This issue is more complex than first meets the eye. For example, the demand for goods increases child labour in the third world in some industries, and hence furthers that practice. At the same time, the use of cheap labour from outside the country increases disadvantage for those people in the first world whose labour is undercut.

41. I have argued that many roles within society have been collapsed and rendered equivalent under the role of consumer. This reduces the value and complexity of roles such as patient, student and citizen, along with roles of doctor, teacher and government. See Long, S. (1999). "The Tyranny of the Customer and the Cost of Consumerism: An analysis using systems and psychoanalytic approaches to groups and society". *Human Relations*, 52 (6): 723–44.

42. This assumption occurs in a form where the group assumes there is no group, only the individual. It seems to be an assumption

underlying some political beliefs, cf. Mrs Thatcher's notion that "there is no society". See Lawrence, W.G., Bain, A. and Gould, L. (1996), op. cit. for a discussion of this basic assumption.

43. Chapman, J. (1999). "Hatred and Corruption of Task". *Socio-Analysis*, 1 (2): 127–50.

44. Stein, M. (2000a). "The Risk Taker as Shadow: A psychoanalytic view of the collapse of Barings bank". *Journal of Management Studies*, 37 (8): 1215–29.

45. Fusaro, P. and Miller, R. (2002). *What Went Wrong at Enron: Everyone's guide to the largest bankruptcy in US history*. USA: Wiley and Sons.

46. Levine, D. (2005), op. cit.

47. Dalgleish, J. and Long, S. (2006). "Management's Fear of Market Demands: A psychodynamic exploration". In: E. Klein and I.L. Pritchard (eds) *Relatedness in a Global Economy*. London: Karnac, pp. 101–23.

48. Chancellor, E. (2002). "Perverse Incentives". *The Australian Financial Review*, 7 June, 2001.

CHAPTER THREE

Perverse Pride

W e are working with a hypothetical; a "what if". What if an organisation were like a person? Or, better put: what if *the system* that is the "organisation" or "corporation" has processes in common with the system that is "person"? That is, human systems, both person and organisation, may have dynamics in common arising from a common systemic root; especially the nature of their emotional content. Or, put in yet another way, the person may be a system where social dynamics are at play on an internal stage, and the organisation a system where emotions are at play on a large collective scale.

The "what if" of this chapter looks at pride. The social nature of pride lies in the recognition of one's qualities or accomplishments by others and an assertion of them by self. A certain amount of pride in one's accomplishments provides a foundation for creative and collaborative work with others. Collective pride provides a strong social glue. But when does pride become arrogance and a sense of self-worth become self-aggrandisement? What makes pride perverse?

To review the idea of perversity, I remind you:

1. The perverse state of mind is not simply a deviation from normative morality. It has to do with individual pleasure at the expense of a more general good. It reflects a state of primary narcissism.
2. The perverse state of mind both acknowledges reality and denies it.

3. The perverse state of mind engages others as accomplices in the perversion, as an extension of the autistic self in support of perverse certainty.
4. The perverse state of mind flourishes where instrumental relations are dominant. This is because instrumentalism treats others as objects and opens up the possibility of abuse which is then ignored. It is a societal state of mind that turns a blind eye.
5. Perversion begets perversion. Abusive cycles are hard to break. Corruption breeds corruption because of the complicity of the accomplices and their subsequent denial and self-deception.

Perverse pride, organisationally speaking, is that state of arrogance that leads organisation members collectively to ignore some of the realities that surround and perhaps threaten them. There is a belief that they are invincible because of their accomplishments or qualities. Moreover, the confidence that comes with such an outlook often convinces others who also want to believe in their invincibility. A collusive pseudo-reality begins to form and becomes invested with all that supports the reputations of those involved, just as in the Hans Christian Andersen tale of the Emperor's new clothes.

A Case of Pride

Financial investment is a gambling game. It is a game of risk where each of the parties involved weighs up their own chances of profit and loss in relation to the risks taken by the other party. It may seem at times to be embedded in logical mathematical analysis but at base it relies on judgements made within a social system of guesses, second guesses, risks and a reliance on social and behavioural trends remaining relatively stable. The big players—the investment banks and financial houses—have the benefits and risks of huge amounts of money to play with. When they win, they win big, and they can win big through the accumulation of a multitude of very small margins. This provides a fertile ground for the development of pride in accomplishment. But, there is also the risk of losing, the stakes are high and new ways to decrease risk and increase takings in the game are constantly sought.

At the beginning of his book on investment strategies—*A Random Walk Down Wall Street*[1]—Malkiel claims that academics and Wall Street traders have a long history of working separately, even shunning each other. For most of the twentieth century, the theories of one were mostly seen as too distant from the real world for the other, and the practices of the other too speculative and short-term oriented for the rational basis of long-term economics. So, what happens then when two Nobel Prize winning economists get together with a group of canny Wall Street traders on the money markets to form a company focused on making a fortune through arbitrage? And what happens when success comes in the turbulent times of the 1980s and 1990s? Chances are you get overwhelming and insurmountable pride.

This is what happened in the lifetime of the investment company Long-Term Capital Management (LTCM). The story told here of LTCM emphasises the belief that its owners had in their own infallibility. The LTCM principals believed that they had found a method of riskless investment. Ignoring any sign to the contrary, their fantasy was that they were modern-day alchemists. Their success led them to be arrogant, contemptuous of others and blind to the real risks they were taking. This pride was bolstered in the belief that they were doing good in the world through making markets more efficient.

The LTCM principals and traders came of age in the Wall Street tradition of machismo demonstrated through clever and successful trading; always being one up on someone else. In this culture, the other side of success was failure and shame.

Some History and Background

John Meriwether was a trader with Salomon Brothers investment bank in the 1970s and 1980s. Salomon's was one of the biggest investment banks in the world. At the time Meriwether joined, trading in shares was the main game. Always part of a gambling game, Salomons in the late twentieth century made an art of taking a pool of bright young business school graduates and training them to work in the short-term world of stock market trading, guessing the future and reading the market. Michael Lewis' book *Liars Poker*[2] tells the story of this time, painting a picture of colourful figures, excessive greed and "macho" wildness as many of these young men made millions of dollars for the company and for themselves. In this world, traders had long been exploiting the possibilities of betting on rises and falls within commodities and stocks through trading futures derivatives, especially through buying or selling options. Options allow buyers to choose to buy (or sell) particular stock in the future at a price set in the present. They have a role in the market as insurance against losses, for example, on commodities.

But, they are open to speculation. Take the case of an option to buy (a call option). When the time comes, if the price has fallen, the buyer has the option not to buy (at the preset higher price). If the price has risen, the buyer profits because s/he can immediately excercise the option—i.e., call on the seller—then sell on the market at the higher price and make a profit. The option seller has the price paid for the option which acts as a hedge against losses in the deals. *He* simply buys the stock at the time the option is called and, if the option were priced right, makes a profit. If no option is called he does nothing but keep the money from the sale of the option. The option is an agreement; a kind of insurance where both buyer and seller can hedge their bets. If working well, all parties seem to gain— at least that's the story. In reality, it is more complex. There are, of course, winners and losers. So, you can imagine that if as a trader you were to buy call options on stock that you guessed would rise, and sell call options on stock that you guessed would fall, you are betting on winning two ways. Moreover, you could buy put options as well which give you the right to sell rather than buy. One thing about the notion of options is that once you think in this way, all sorts of bets, guesses and agreements can be made into options. The interest is not in the stock themselves, but in their volatility; their rises and falls in price. So anything that has this sort of volatility is open to options trading.

One snag was the difficulty faced in the pricing of options (the hedging strategy) so that they were a reasonable investment in the gambling process involved and competitive in the market. If a trader could price options more accurately than another, they would have an advantage. Outside of Wall Street, the pricing of options was a problem being tackled by academic economists.

Meriwether was interested in trading in bonds. A major feature of government bonds is that they provide, for general investors, a relatively low risk form of investment. They are backed by governments and mature at fixed times and provide fixed interest rates. Meriwether was interested in bonds not for the realisation of a final real value, but because of their connection to interest rates. The value of bonds goes up when interest rates go down and vice versa. In the changing times of the 1980s international currencies were no longer fixed to a standard but were floating in relation to one another. In conjunction with this, interest rates also floated. That is, there was volatility in the space between different currencies. In this context it seemed that money could be made simply in the gaps between securities relative to one another and in the different interest rates offered by different governments. For instance, the investment banks were able to collect fees in brokeraging agreements for swaps between different investors from different countries. These investors were able to take advantage of the low interest rates offered them within their own countries and, through a swap agreement with an investor from a different country, were able to get the lower rates there also. This opened new doors for the banks themselves, far beyond mere brokerage. If options could be taken out on interest rates not just stocks, then the fabled golden egg of arbitrage risk-free profit could be laid by the seeming plain bonds goose.

Within Salomons, Meriwether formed a group that took up the goose. The interest rates and bonds markets were vast beyond commodities and shares. He recruited bright graduates from business and economics but also paid attention to the professors who were working on models to price a whole range of options, especially options in the bonds market. He brought the academic work right to the bonds trading floor. He and his group were confident that they now had the solution to options pricing and thus were risk-free.

In addition, when pricing options, a process called the delta hedge was discovered. In this process risk is reduced by ensuring that an investment portfolio includes a relative number of options alongside owned stocks and bonds. This was called the "replicating portfolio". Nicholas Dunbar[3] explains:

> Regardless of whether the stock goes up or down, the value of your portfolio in a month will be the same ... the existence of this "replicating portfolio" is the reason why the option price depends on volatility, but not the stock price return. Higher

volatility leads to a higher options price because it is harder for the replicating portfolio to break even when the stock price changes rapidly.[4]

The 1980s were proving to be volatile times and Meriwether, his traders and academics (called quants) became good at pricing options on bonds of all kinds. They were discovering more and more arbitrage situations that indicated riskless profit. Their confidence was growing. Within Salomons they became increasingly profitable and concomitantly powerful. All this helped Meriwether's group and their clients following the disastrous stock market crash of 1987. They were trading bonds rather than stock and they were trading options. With the combination of intellectual economists who built successful statistical and mathematical models for predicting and extracting any spare money in the markets through their arbitrage practices, and market savvy traders who found hidden arbitrage in practically every kind of money market product or agreement, the group was amassing huge profits.

By 1990 the arbitrage group within Salomons, although relatively small in number (about 100 people) were bringing in as much money as the larger part of the company who were traditional investment bankers (around 6,000 people). Meriwether expected each of his traders to bring in at least $6 million a year. With such high earnings, the traders and their academic advisors were well rewarded and were given unprecedented salaries and bonuses reaching into the millions. Meriwether himself rose to Vice President. By any standard, they were a huge success. But there was more to come. Additional leveraging (i.e., borrowing more money) on top of basic equity rapidly increased profits. This all seemed the natural thing to do. If you could make small very safe profits from a relatively small base, why not leverage that so that more capital was available to make all these small safe profits become large ones. It all seemed so easy.

Greed is one of the corporate sins (see Chapter 4). Salomons itself might be a case study in point here. Despite the fact that many of these new money markets deals were done "off the books" over the counter and evaded taxation, the company's accountants and traders worked to find more and more ways to get around large tax bills. What eventually led to disaster was the violation of US government trading rules on the proportion of new bonds that could be purchased by any one buyer. When this violation came to light and Salomons was threatened with exclusion from US bond sales, Salomons went close to bankruptcy. Nicholas Dunbar, whose work I have heavily drawn from in this account, is not able to give account as to why the Bank's President did not move swiftly to get rid of Nicholas Mozer, the Salomon's trader at the root of the illegal trading once he was caught out on one illegal trade. His excuse was not convincing, but he was permitted to remain at Salomons for another four months before the scandal of the extent of the further illegal trading broke out.

By this time Meriwether was the Vice President and his own success did not earn him friends in all parts of the company, despite his popularity at the arbitrage desk. In the fall-out of the illegal trading fiasco Meriwether was sacked, not specifically through his own practice, but because of the behaviour of one of his subordinates. Mozer was one of his chief traders. Envy, yet another of those deadly sins, might well have played a part in his downfall and we can well imagine that Meriwether was humiliated and shamed in the process. Pride, greed and envy linked arms in this story. But, Salomons is not the story to focus on here. I need to move to the story of LTCM. It just had its roots in Salomon's proud and successful arbitrage group.

LTCM

Meriwether formed a hedge fund, LTCM in 1993 together with several other of the old Salomon's group. Hedging is a process whereby you "hedge" the stock that you want, by finding stock that you don't want, but think is overpriced, and selling it "short". This means that instead of having to buy or put up the money at the time of the deal, you sell stock that you have borrowed. When the price falls you buy the same stock on the market and return it to the person who loaned it to you together with interest, all paid with the profit you made. This profit acts as an insurance against losses made on the stock you actually want. It acts as an overall insurance of a stock portfolio. But, nonetheless, it is a bet on the price moving.

This style of betting became popular in the derivatives markets in the 1980s and 1990s. Beyond betting on stock was the betting on currencies and interest rates. In many ways, buying an option for a currency or interest rate exchange is like paying the interest up-front. Except, the option could also be bought and sold throughout its life. Even more complex were "swaptions" which are options to do an interest rate swap including "caps" and "floors" put on floating interest rates. All these new forms of agreement: options, swaps, swaptions were popular during the rapidly changing social and political climate. European currencies moving towards the common European monetary system provided opportunities for arbitrage. Eventually these currencies were to converge in the one value so bets could be made on which countries would eventually join the common monetary system. The breakdown of the iron curtain, rise of some Asian economies, increasing global economy and multi-national status of companies all provided the impetus for foreign investments and chances for dealing in the bond markets of foreign governments.

Meriwether quickly raised capital for LTCM from investors on the strength of his past performance.

In raising funds Meriwether created the category of *Strategic Investors*, who would invest at least $100 million. He was successful in bringing in some of the top financial organisations in the world into LTCM despite the fact that the fees charged were exceptionally high. The typical hedge funds charged 20 per cent of profits earned plus one per cent of an investor's assets as fees. In contrast LTCM charged 25 per cent of profits and levied a 2 per cent fee on assets. In addition, investors in LTCM were required to commit their funds for at least three years. Despite the heavy fees and long-term commitment LTCM was able to raise $1.25 billion.[5] This indicates the extent of the faith that these banks, governments and financiers had in Meriwether and his team.

Two of the original partners in LMTC were Myron Scholes and Robert Merton. These two former academic economists were to receive a Nobel Prize in economics in 1977 for their work on pricing options. Merton's focus lay with building profit from the power of arbitrage which, he emphasised, enforced cheap pricing. Part of LTCM's success became built on its traders finding mispriced securities.

LTCM's main strategy was to make convergence trades. These trades involved finding securities that were mispriced relative to one another, taking long positions in the cheap ones and short positions in the rich ones. Because these differences in values were tiny, the fund needed to take large and highly leveraged positions in order to make a significant profit.[6] The point of leverage was that they could take half a per cent here and half a per cent there over and above the interest they paid on debt. But, they believed they could continue to do this with no risk.

The company had developed complex mathemetical models to take advantage of fixed income arbitrage deals (termed convergence trades) usually with US, Japanese and European government bonds. The basic idea was that over time the value of long-dated bonds issued a short time apart would tend to become identical. However, the rate at which these bonds approached this price would be different, and that more heavily traded bonds such as the US Treasury bonds would approach the long-term price more quickly than less heavily traded and less liquid bonds ... it would be possible to make a profit as the difference in the value of the bonds converged.[7]

The academic economists with their mathematical skills and theories, and now, thanks to Meriwether's inclusion of them at Salomon's, their own market experience, were a key ingredient in the whole success of LTCM in its heyday. They provided the models that formed the basis of what were known as "money making machines". Dunbar describes a mortgage bond money machine. "This machine is a leveraged, top-heavy contraption containing not just the bond, but also Treasury futures, swaps and dozens of interest rate options, each of which click into action and out again at different points in time".[7a] New machines were created for new situations, new products and new deals. In order to create, run and maintain these virtual machines a whole body of PhD graduates, traders and risk managers were employed.

Clearly taking a gamble, this business requires skill at spotting overpriced securities, predicting interest rate changes and brokering deals with and between couterparties who also stand to profit from the transactions. Built in also were the risk management strategies built on delta hedging. LTCM did all this with its combination of experienced traders, money machine developers and support from the Wall Street establishment and was making huge profits. Investors were keen to invest and some were highly disappointed when they were unable to buy shares in the company. It seemed that LTCM was able to find the "money for nothing" sung about by the pop group Dire Straits in 1985. That song was about the excesses of pop stars. Between 1993 and 1998 the principals of LTCM themselves became excessively rich.

Done on a large scale, it seems, all this should have a strong underlying asset base or equity. But players in the game were highly leveraged; LTCM at about 40 per cent. That is, their actual assets (money, stocks or bonds) were small compared to the mass of loans that they carried forward in the various arbitrage deals that were made on a daily basis. LTCM was the most highly leveraged of all. *Yet no one was concerned.* LTCM was respected by the big investment banks and found no trouble in gaining loans to support its dealings. That is, they had easy access to liquidity. Moreover, some of the risk strategies usually employed by these banks were lowered or dismissed in dealings with LTCM.

> The people at LTCM drove very hard bargains on financing. They were able to get low rates and special deals because the banks did not want to get left out of LTCM business. LTCM was reputed to have a sure fire way to make fabulous profits and to be paying $100 million a year in finance fees. No banker wanted to be left out of that bonanza.[8]

But in 1998 huge problems arose. In particular, large investments in Russian Government bonds were lost when the Russian Government was unable to make its treasury repayments and the Russian banks that were used to hedge the deals collapsed. Beyond this, there was a "run to liquidity" in the global markets as the extent of Russia's financial problems increased. LTCM's hedging strategies collapsed. They joined the run to liquidity, sold off their more liquid assets and were left with only long-term illiquid assets. No longer able to buy liquidity from other investment banks who were facing similar issues, they were unable to pay their own debts. Eventually, they were bailed out by a consortium of banks supported by the US government and wound down over the next couple of years. Why was this private company bailed out? Because their leverage had been so large, their dealings so complex (none of their major lenders knew exactly who else they were dealing with, much of this was kept secret) and the network of their involvement in the financial markets so extensive that their bankruptcy threatened global markets.

Written case study reports refer to the lessons to be learned from the fall of LTCM after markets fell in 1998 primarily in terms of the economic and business processes involved. They refer to the problems of excessive leverage and a failure to appreciate that full hedging is not possible at those times when there are unpredictable extreme jumps in the market, such as happened with Russia. The money machines of LTCM were based on "fair market prices", that is, the prices that would be there when markets converged back to their normal states. However, in times of crisis, investors and shareholders want to draw on actual market prices, not long-term possibilities. This is when liquidity is critical. If the company does not have the money or equity to draw on, high losses ensue. This is what happened with LTCM:

> Illiquid securities are marked-to-market; margin calls are made; the illiquid securities must be sold; more margin calls are made, and so on. In general, shareholders may provide patient capital; but debt-holders do not.[9]

What LTCM principals believed to be "fail-safe" money making machines were based on flawed assumptions that markets were frictionless and continuous. The assumption of frictionlessness was in relation to costs. For small players, the cost of transactions and the taxes related to transactions cause friction. They are significant costs. For large players such as the investment banks and hedge funds they prove minimal, so the assumption is accepted. The assumption of continuous markets means that you can trade as often as you want and in as large quantities as you wish. It also assumes the associated factors of being able to borrow as much as you need at risk-free interest rates. This is an assumption of continuous liquidity. Again, this holds most of the time for the large institutions who are able to borrow from each other and, at times, corner the market as LTCM did in the case of Italian Government bonds. The size of these trading giants renders these assumptions workable, for the most part, under most conditions.

The third assumption was that the money making machines have a normal curve to describe their returns. Dunbar argues that the normality assumption was challenged during the crash in 1987. The assumption of liquidity was challenged during the fall of LTCM in

1998. The economic and political situation shook the bonds market and the money machines became useless as LTCM's liquidity failed.

But what are the explanations of human emotion behind these failures?

The Human Decisions

I quoted Malkiel at the beginning of this chapter and return to him here. He describes two approaches to stock market trading. These he calls the "solid foundation" approach and the "castles in the air" approach. The solid foundation approach basically says that investors should find and invest in good solid companies that provide better than inflation returns over the long term. Judgements can be made by studying performance over time and the reasons behind why companies rise and fall on the stock market. Fluctuations over the short term can be ignored. (Betting on these is no better than a monkey throwing darts at the financial pages of a newspaper to find an investment strategy.) He links Warren Buffett, the Omaha investment guru to this approach.

The second approach, the "castles in the air" approach, is focused more on human psychology. This approach to investment says that you have to read how the market will respond to events because it is not the intrinsic worth of companies or stock that is important, but their market price. The approach involves reading how other investors will be reading the market because they will respond to their own reading of how others will respond. This argument can become an infinite regress of second guessing. But rather than a major focus on long-term risks, this approach attempts to get returns also in the short term. While reading the market can be an art, and while there is no argument that human psychology plays a major role in how prices jump around, the short-term approach ignores the fluctuations that may come from a variety of unpredictable circumstances beyond a simple approach to the dynamics of human choice.

LTCM was closely coupled to the pay offs between short- and long-term investments. Their successes were due to playing with so much liquidity in the short term that they could find free money in the cracks of the worldwide financial system. It's a bit like the fantasy every child seems to have at some time: namely, if everyone in the country just gave me one (unwanted or unneeded) cent, I'd be rich.

Myron Scholes stated the objective of LTCM in a striking image. He said LTCM would function like a giant vacuum cleaner sucking up nickels that everyone else had overlooked.[10]

He and his partners were clever. They had the knowledge of how to do this, the confidence of investment banks and governments who would invest or lend them the money to make it work and they had the opportunities through LTCM. As long as the assumptions behind their money machines held, and they didn't doubt them, they rode the waves of success. As indication of their philosophy of being able to read the market through using derivatives, they put much of their business into betting on the convergence of European currencies and bonds hedged by US dollars. This seemed a good bet, but it led to too many proverbial eggs in the basket. Many deals rested on the same type of guesses that they thought were foolproof. They were clever, confident and their pride led them to a fall.

Take the following situation. By 1997 returns for investors, although still good, were down on the 1995 and 1996 figures. In early 1998, LTCM returned $2.7 billion of equity to investors. Why? Meriwether and his colleagues didn't want LTCM to become a large organisation trading equities like Salomons. This would be boring and beneath them. They were pleased with their unregulated status and huge leverage off small equity. They confidently believed they had liquidity through their relations with the banks, international investors and their hedging policies. The investors were amazed and disgruntled. Who gives investment monies back? LTCM principals didn't want the investment of others. Returns were going down, not up. They could better use borrowed capital in arbitrage trades.

Dunbar reports Scholes as stating that systematic hedging was as safe as having equity as a risk cushion and that in the future more corporations would move to this and hence towards increasing privately held, as against publically traded, shares.[11] They were riding high on their arbitrage bets and didn't want to invest in new endeavours. By this time all the principals and most of the traders had invested their personal fortunes in the business. They thought there was no risk; they had it all in hand.

Stein[12] provides a tight argument about why the failure of LTCM was not simply due to their inability to access or comprehend information relating to risk factors that theories of rational process within organisations postulate. He argues that LTCM displayed characteristics of organisational narcissism that became built into their socio-technical systems, including their risk management structures, from the outset. He outlines five components of organisational narcissism. First, there is an exaggerated pride where the organisation is felt to be flawless. Second, there is an associated unconscious omnipotence "unable to tolerate the autonomous existence of anything of value outside itself".[13] Third, a belief exists in its own omniscience, its capacity to know everything it needs to. Fourth, these delusions of omnipotence and omniscience are accompanied by "dismissiveness and triumphal contempt" of others.[14] Finally, Stein poses that these characteristics are permanently built into the structures and functions of the organisation in an institutionalised fashion. This organisational narcissism, Stein argues, led LTCM partners to take extreme risks.

The Nature of Pride

For psychoanalysts, pride begins with the body: what it is and what it is able to produce. An infant will take pride in mastery of movement and in its capacity to communicate. Perhaps the first signs of pride are recognised through a triumphant crowing or glee that mother can share. The toddler increases her abilities and proudly asserts herself. Every parent can recognise the infant's discovery of "no" or "won't" as a strong sign of such assertion. The social imperative to control the body becomes focused on cleanliness and toilet training and pride in accomplishment grows as first the body and later the mind produces "products" of value: faeces in the toilet, drawings and playthings in the playroom and words and thoughts in conversation. Later still, pride becomes attached to one's gender, sexual and social identity as the toddler becomes preschooler and the whole issue of physical differences in sexual anatomy is approached along with erotic longings. Freudians see this development primarily in terms of sexual development through oral, anal, phallic and latency periods. Pride can be integrally linked to how this development proceeds but always with a link into the body.

We learn pride in ourselves and our accomplishments early in life at our mother's knee. Parents are influential in helping their children to gain a healthy sense of pride or self-respect. When mother or father's eyes light up and they say "aren't you clever!" to their child or "he's so helpful" or "she really is smart" to someone else, the toddler begins to see him or herself with the same sort of pride that the parent feels. Pride begins when the child is able to see his own accomplishments, abilities or qualities as valued in the eyes of important others.

The other side of this is shame. Shame is felt if accomplishments, abilities and qualities are felt to be inferior, or worse, despicable. This sense of pride or shame reaches far beyond one's abilities and accomplishments to the very foundation of feelings about the self. Although the advice of psychologist Carl Rogers was to distinguish between unconditional love of the child and disapproval of some of his or her actions, advice earlier given by St Peter, this is not as easily done as said. A sense of self-loathing on the one hand can come from the shame felt as others point out our failings. On the other hand, self-aggrandisement can come from unrealistic pride—perhaps when pride is used to defend against shame or is based not on real accomplishment but on a distorted picture given by those who wish to flatter.

Adlerians speak of the superiority and inferiority complexes; names given to the extremes of pride and shame in inner experience.[15] Adler claimed that the central drive in life involves a future-orientation towards a significant goal, superiority or success. This goal may be unconscious and not obvious to the individual, but may be found, he argues, through understanding the roots of one's typical coping patterns, the influence of social and cultural factors, and, primarily, through discovery of one's own creative powers that bring together various influences and shape unique character structure. For healthy, stable individuals the life goal is realised as a socially useful and realistically achievable goal.[16] For some, though, it becomes unrealistic or a driving wish to be superior despite indications that this is impossible or destructive.

Adler theorised a need to compensate for the natural inferiority experienced as a small child in a world of stronger, cleverer adults. The shame of inferiority, first felt by the child in relation to physical and intellectual stature, leads to a contempt for the self which can be transferred to others. When feelings of inferiority are predominant, or when the compensating attitudes of arrogance or exaggerated superiority emerge, a narcissistic character develops. This character is more likely to be exploitative of others than empathic. It is a character full of pride built on the need to disqualify the capacity of the other. At an extreme it can become a pathological delusion of grandeur, masking the underlying fear of being nothing.

The initial, perhaps realistic sense of inferiority may be moderated at first through a supportive family system that helps the child come to value self and other through mutual respect. Such an approach develops a community orientation and more realistic character structure that may be strengthened later through the social institutions in which the individual lives and works. The capacity for connection to the wider community Adler sees as critical. It is within the connectedness of relationship that a deep sense of belonging, inherently desired, can be achieved. This may be through love and sex, work or other forms of relationship.

This snapshot shows that exaggerated pride may be a compensatory mechanism for shame. Such an idea can be found in other theories. The object relations theorists see pride as a defence against shame. It is as if there is a continuum where shame is at one pathological end, exaggerated pride at the other and in the middle is the healthy position where self-worth is linked to creative striving and service to others. I take up Adler's ideas at this point because of the link he provides between pride, shame and the community.[17] The modulation of pride and shame comes from connectedness to a broader community. LTCM was a closed, narcissistic and individualistic culture. It grew from the broader culture of Wall Street where shame was used and feared and arrogance developed as traders rose through the ranks.

The Social Character of Pride and Shame

What I want most to emphasise in this chapter is not the development of pride as an individual characteristic, although it is expressed through the attitudes and stances of individuals. I am interested in how pride operates within a group or organisation. Pride and shame can be seen as integrally linked to the development of the psyche within the social and communal context. This follows from the psychoanalytic formulations of pride.

First, the importance of the body is recognised. Pride or shame is felt very directly in bodily sensations. We say someone is "puffed up with importance and pride" or we may blush with shame or wish to hide our bodies from the sight of others. Although this embodiment may seem a very individual characteristic of pride and shame, the bodily response is critical in terms of the communication of social relatedness between the shamed and the shamer. Intensely felt by the individual, the public signs of pride and shame in the body play a critical role in the culture of the group.

This leads to the second point. Pride and shame are feelings generated within the public sphere. We feel ashamed when our inadequacies are exposed or we are unable to perform to the expectations of others. We feel the glow of pride when our accomplishments are recognised and lauded by others. Although we may well harbour a hidden internal sense of pride in self, this is exceedingly hard to maintain if the opinions and attitudes of others towards us fail to reinforce this or actively work against it. The feelings of those who become unemployed for long periods of time attest to this. In a world where employment is critical to identity and sense of self-worth, feelings of shame quickly emerge when it seems that no one else values what you have or are. Moreover, shame may be felt as a result of context where one is seen to be outside the norm or as the result of identification with a group or organisation which, itself, becomes shameful in the eyes of the wider society, or is felt to be.[18]

Erik Erikson pointed out that some societies are based on shame and others on guilt as psychological methods for controlling their members.[19] Those based on shame predominantly use public exposure and punishment as censure, rather than relying on the individual's own inner conscience as a regulatory device. Many societies are based on a mixture of shame and guilt. The media in our society, for instance, can easily act as a modern-day pillory. A redundancy notice or being publically escorted from the building (as were many LTCM employees following their failure) may act in a way similar to a public whipping through the high street.

A third point is that pride and shame are closely linked to the person's sense of agency or the ability to assert or proclaim self in the face of others. Pride and shame work as a social hierarchy. There is a power relation or a relation of dominance involved. Those who can be proud stand high above those who have been shamed. This is obvious in the practice of slavery. Societies that took slaves found an economic advantage in this practice it's true, but the taking of slaves was also a move to shame the beaten opponent and hence heighten the sense of pride and dominance of the victors. A strong sense of triumph is evident. The same dynamic is true in the triumphs surrounding trading deals.

That arrogance and triumph are defences against shame is a fourth and critical point. Those who wish to distance themselves from the shamed, because their own shame may be exposed, become more arrogant. This defence works in a perverse way; as a mask that hides an uneasy fear, yet constantly exposes it because the wearer of the mask needs to see that which he is afraid of in the other. Certainty masks the fear of not knowing; dominance masks the fear of weakness. The arrogant need others to be shamed, lest their contempt is turned inward. Arrogance is an aggressive posture, giving rise to aggressive acts. Bion claims,[20] "in the personality where life instincts predominate, pride becomes self-respect, where death instincts predominate, pride becomes arrogance". LTCM principals were driven by their wish to make money, but also by their righteousness; that they knew *best of all* in the investing world.

These four points:

1. the individual (or group) bodily expression;
2. the social cause of pride and shame,
3. their relation to social domination and,
4. the perverse defensive nature of arrogance

have a place in the LTCM story. They are displayed in how the partners presented themselves to the world, how they kept themselves secretive and contemptuous of others, including their own employees, and how they developed those characteristics of a perverse organisation: they involve denial and blindness.

Pride and the Phallic Culture of Wall Street

Although often characterised as "pure greed", the culture of the Wall Street investment bank players in the 1980s and 1990s, especially those in the derivatives and futures markets might be understood as a culture of pride and shame. The recipe for such a climate included the following mix. First in the mix is a hierarchy of market wise dealers used to placing large bets in a volatile market situation.

The trading floor led them to be brash, loud, fast and accustomed to making decisions amid a complex set of factors. Following the "castles in the air" philosophy, they believed that success came with second guessing others and finding the next sucker to come along.

Second, there was a continuous influx of young (mostly) men, spilling out from business schools, MBAs hot in their hands, highly motivated to succeed. The image of testosterone directed towards playing the market is perhaps apt. Third in the mix was a competitive atmosphere, not simply between different institutions but within any one institution, to go where the money and power was and to rise through the ranks. The cleverness, competitive attitude and testosterone all combined into an attitude of arrogance often mixed with contempt for those seen as "lesser"; with fear and awe of those who made the big deals. The name given to the latter, "big swinging dick", is indicative of the image of machismo.[21] At least this was how it was on the surface.

The description of the pride exhibited in this culture is quite unavowedly phallic. It is a collective version of the individual "swagger". The mortgage bond traders in the 1980s and the arbitrage traders in the 1990s were paid far more than the already well paid equities traders and other investment bankers. Young men in their twenties were making millions of dollars a year as well as getting bonuses. Lewis describes the Salomon mortgage bond traders in the 1980s. His description bespeaks the arrogant attitude bred of perverse wealth.

> The department, in short, looked more like a fraternity than it did the division of a large corporation. The boss was at least partly responsible for the adolescent nature of his department. He wasn't just one of the boys; he was the ringleader ... Skewered by the mail spear on Ranieri's trading desk were an orange pair of stripper's panties ... Andy Stone recalls having a bottle of Bailey's Irish Cream poured into his jacket pockets by Ranieri. When he complained that it was his favorite suit, Ranieri whipped out four soiled hundred dollar bills and said, "Don't complain, buy a new one!"[22]

Although this was the extreme end of Wall Street culture, it shows how small sections that make huge profits and satisfy the corporation's greed can grow an inflated opinion of their worth. Outrageous behaviour accompanied almost pornographic displays of wealth. Throughout his description, Lewis shows how the arrogance was bred in a culture of domination. If you were not good enough you were soon cast out. Shame, loss of face and failure were the other side of the trading coin. Those higher up the hierarchy of trading often held those below in contempt, until they could prove themselves in large deals. It was a picture of superior and inferior; master and slave exaggerated in the bond trading desks. At least that was the myth that underpinned the culture.

In reality, investment bankers for the most part took small risks. Large deals could be earned through a multitude of small deals on a vast equity. The smaller group of swaggerers was on the margin, albeit the rich margin that allowed them to be pampered while all went well. But as we have seen, the story was different at LTCM where the huge equity of Salomon's was replaced by the false certainty of money machines.

The Pride of LTCM

The culture of pride that had been internalised by the Bonds arbitrage group at Salomon's was intensified in the short life of LTCM. Meriwether was able to gather together those traders who had previously worked successfully with him. Moreover, he had learned not to simply train up young MBA graduates with a yearning for the big times, but was bringing on a more serious academic coterie of economics PhDs to help develop the mathematical models needed for Merton's and Scholes' economic theories. LTCM also had two Nobel Prize winners and David Mullins who had been appointed previously to the Federal Reserve as Vice President by President Bush. Their reputation was more than good; their pride high.

Dunbar reports: "According to one of London's top swaps dealers, working for a US investment bank, 'Long Term had a real arrogant streak.'"[23] He also quotes this dealer as saying "I think there were two kinds of people they wanted to deal with. One was people who were as smart as they were but just had a different mindset about how they used their brains; who were just going to give liquidity ... The other people Long Term liked to deal with were the idiots, who could be picked off routinely."[24]

This gives some indication of the state of mind present in LTCM's culture. It was this state of mind that led to the decision to return investment monies. It was this state of mind that led to an ill-fated belief in the assumptions that underpinned their "money machines" and gave the impression of invulnerability. The description of the players that I have gleaned in my reading seems no longer that of the adolescent phallic swagger, such as described by Lewis in Salomon's. It is a picture of apparently cool, clear, hard traders. The handling of their Italian deal,[25] where, as a result of dealings with the Italian Government many local Italian insurance companies and superannuation funds suffered huge losses, consequently leading to the ruin of many small companies and people, provides a story of ruthless pursuit of self-glory.[26]

Pride lay in an ability to convince their counterparties, finding new trades and deals that would lay aside doubt. The image is one of domination at a global level; players across a range of governments and multinational investment banks. Often described as nice guys in themselves, the culture was one of domination with others seen as objects to be manipulated.

Stein describes this as organisational narcissism[27] and demonstrates how unconscious processes fuelled risky behaviour by the partners. His point is that these were neither rational risks nor risks driven simply by acquisitiveness or greed. The unconscious motivation sprang from hubris, associated delusions of grandeur, omnipotence, omniscience and triumph over others.

However, I would take this beyond narcissism. There is here a picture of clearly perverse pride. It fits with the signs of perversion noted previously:

1. Arrogant pride with an inward looking *narcissistic stance is evident*. They had an inflated image of their own significance, power and knowledge and grew to have contempt for many of their competitors and counterparties.
2. *Denial* of the possibility that their assumptions could be wrong was paired with knowledge that they did have of the risks they were taking. They could go with the denial because they believed in a fail-safe hedging. Remember, as long as the assumptions behind their money machines held, and they didn't doubt them, they rode the waves of success.

3. *Knowing and yet not knowing* the risks they played with. Brimelow[28] says, "they acknowledged but ignored the fact that probability distributions in financial markets often show 'fat tails'—in other words that extreme events occur far more frequently than a normal curve would predict." They came to believe that systematic hedging was as good as having equity, yet they also knew that they were flying in the face of usual sound practice.

4. *Using others as accomplices and collaborators* in the abuse of third parties. Many major banks continued to believe in them, even without knowledge or understanding of their situation and practices. Of the financial institution counterparties, Lowenstein, cited by Brimelow[29] says

> through their carelessness, their reckless financing, their vain attempts to ingratiate themselves with a self important client, the Wall Street banks had created this fiasco together ... they too, were awed by ... the partners' reputation, degrees and celebrity.

Even governments collaborated with them as in the case of the Italian Government.

> Dunbar directly asserts ... that the Italian authorities in effect hired LTCM to groom or manipulate the Italian bond market, in order to accelerate convergence with the other European Monetary System bond markets and to reduce the Italian government interest burden.[30]

5. *Thriving in a culture of instrumentality* where trading depends more on finding disparities in pricing than in finding intrinsic value; where employees were treated by the partners with contempt.

6. Modelling and breeding contempt within the Wall Street culture. A whole culture followed the flawed assumptions of Merton and Scholes taken up in LTCM.

A critical aspect in the picture of perversion, beyond elements of narcissism, are the wider social implications. Others become drawn into the sphere of perversity. Narcissism is often a characteristic of the isolated individual or organisation caught hopelessly in their own delusions. Perversity requires accomplices.

As it was, the LTCM partners personally lost their fortunes and came close to bringing disaster to the world money markets. Even in their demise, they drew in the large financial institutions. The web of involvement was so intricately intertwined between them and they believed they were right.

We can ask the question of how self-respect and normal pride become exaggerated and perverse? How is it the sight of real risk is lost? The answers that I have considered here include a social defence against the experience of shame underpinned by a desire to achieve dominance at the expense of others. Denigration and attendant shame were often conditions of being for those who peopled the lower echelons of Wall Street culture. Triumph over that was evident in the perverse pride of LTCM. This is a perverse position which Bion links with the death drive, and which Hegel, Lacan and Benjamin would regard as a reflection of a primitive human struggle. Adler's notion of the desire to belong poses a paradox. The stronger the sense of belonging to (and identifying with) the sub-group, the stronger the possibility of rejection of the wider group. LTCM traders felt a very strong sense of belonging to their own group which supported their blindness to the larger system. Lowenstein claims that each deal was focused on in isolation, pursued by a partner bent on making a large profit without a sense of the bigger picture. It is a picture of a closed-off narcissistic system that eventually led to perverse practice.

Notes

1. Malkiel, B.G. (2003). *A Random Walk Down Wall Street: The time-tested strategy for successful investing*. NY: W.W. Norton.
2. Lewis, M. (1990). *Liar's Poker*. London: Coronet Books.
3. Dunbar, N. (2001). *Inventing Money: The story of Long-Term Capital Management and the legends behind it*. NY: John Wiley and Sons.
4. Ibid., p. 36.
5. www.applet-magic.com/ltcm.htm.
6. Wikipedia, the free encyclopedia, 2006.
7. Dunbar, N. (2001), op. cit., p. 127.
7a. Ibid.

8. www.applet-magic.com/ltcm.htm.
9. www.erisk.com/Learning/CaseStudies/ref_case_ltcm.asp.
10. www.applet-magic.com/ltcm.htm.
11. Dunbar, N. (2001), op. cit., pp. 198–9.
12. Stein, M. (2003). "Unbounded Irrationality: Risk and organizational narcissism at Long Term Capital Management". *Human Relations*, 56 (5): 523–40.
13. Ibid., p. 529.
14. Ibid., p. 530.
15. Adler, A. (1912). "*The Neurotic Character*". In: *The Collected Clinical Works of Alfred Adler Volume 1* (2003). Alfred Adler Institute of Northwestern Washington.
16. Adler, A. (1998). *Social Interest*. Revised edition. London: Oneworld Publications.
17. Erik Erikson later develops similar ideas in his theory of psycho-social development. Erikson, E.H. (1950). *Childhood and Society*. London and NY: W.W. Norton.
18. Both Hunt, J.M., "Organisational Leadership and Shame" www.ispso.org/Symposia/London/2000hunt.htm. and Flynn, R., "Impediments to Organisational Effectiveness—social defences and shame in the workplace". *Socio-Analysis*, 3 (2): 109–22, discuss shame in terms of the identification of people with their workplace organisations.
19. Erikson, E.H. (1950), op. cit.
20. Bion, W.R. (1967). *Second Thoughts*. London: Karnac Books, p. 84.
21. Lewis, M. (1990), op. cit.
22. Ibid., p. 144.
23. Dunbar, N. (2001), op. cit., p. 154.
24. Ibid., p. 158.
25. Ibid., pp. 150–62.
26. The US Government's capping of bond sales and violation of this had led indirectly to Meriwether's leaving Salomons. Now LTCM, with the collaboration of the Italian Government successfully cornered a government bond market. This demonstrates the proud triumph of LTCM traders over the shame of the past.
27. Stein, M. (2003), op. cit.
28. Brimelow, J. (2004). *Review of "When Genius Failed" by Robert Lowenstein*. www.vdare.com/jb/ltcm.htm.
29. Ibid., p. 9.
30. Cf. www.vdare.com/pb/WallStChangingCulture.htm.

CHAPTER FOUR

Perverse Greed

When thinking of big multinational corporations and corruption the idea of greed is often foremost in our minds. Media stories of Enron, Worldcorp (in USA), Parmalat (in Italy) and HIH (in Australia) for instance, often focus on what seems to be the intent of senior executives who have huge salaries plus shares and other financial interests in the company or its future. Stories of fraud, lies and cover-ups, where the company's true financial status is hidden from the market, abound and confirm our cynicism about big business being a potential breeding ground for greedy and exploitative executives and board members.

Of course, the stories are more complex than the image that "pure greed" conveys. Issues of pride and arrogance are present. A blind eye is turned, at times, to obvious incompetence in people with power and influence and to information that runs counter to what is desired.[1] Checks and balances in risk assessment are overstepped and ignored in a flush of confidence and single mindedness. There is a belief in being right; even in being righteous.[2] Hubristic decisions are made that over-reach or over-extend the resources of the company. Then, when mistakes are gradually recognised because the reality of their effects can no longer be ignored, frantic attempts to bail out or cover-up come into play. Greed is but one factor in the whole picture.

But, it is an important factor. It is worth exploring the nature of greed and how it comes into play in organisational life. Less forgivable than pride or hubris in the popular mind, greed seems to epitomise an ignoble, rampant self-indulgence. It implies taking more than you need from the common pot, leaving others, often employees, shareholders and customers, with less. Pride, when positive and on the side of the life forces can be seen as a form of self-respect and generativity. Greed has little to recommend itself. It is often hidden and secretive, hoarding and anal. Avarice is the term in the parlance of deadly sins. And when not hidden, its overt display has overtones of indecency and obscene sensuality. Gluttony and rampant lust are also called to mind.

Parmalat and the Greedy CEO

The story of the fall of the giant dairy corporation Parmalat gripped newspaper headlines in 2004. The story had at its centre a godfather-like figure of larger-than-life stature, and all the elements of a tragic drama. It was a story to fit the popular view of individual greed hidden beneath power and respectability.

On Sunday January 2004, *Time Magazine* ran a story on Calisto Tanzi, CEO of Parmalat, an Italian-based multinational dairy producer. The article begins:

> From Milan boardrooms to Parma dairy farms, Calisto Tanzi has long been viewed as the model Italian entrepreneur: hardworking, successful, modest, pious and, above all, generous. Over the past four decades, as he built dairy company Parmalat into a worldwide giant with annual sales of €7.6 billion, he showered his hometown of Parma with his philanthropy. Tanzi helped pay for a major restoration of Parma's theater and 11th century basilica. He poured cash into the local soccer team, making it one of Europe's best, and financed programs for the poor, aids patients and drug addicts. Last February, when the Catholic Church was looking for funds to renovate a mountain clinic for asthmatic children, Monsignor Franco Grisenti only needed to ask, and his old friend Tanzi, 65, immediately made an interest-free loan of €400,000. "He's got that impulse in him to just say yes," the prelate marvels.[3]

Tanzi founded Parmalat in 1961 after his father died and he inherited the family prosciutto factory. A visit to Sweden led him to see the benefits of packaging milk in cartons rather than bottles. Back in Italy he took up this idea, introduced a process for producing long-life milk and quickly built the company into a billion dollar food giant. The company grew to having annual sales of $9 billion with 36,000 employees in over 30 countries.

But in November 2004, a scandal broke out that led to Tanzi's eventual house arrest for alledged embezzlement and fraud. A failure to go through with a $400 million bond issue raised the alarm. One by one, several directors resigned. First the CFO Fausto Tonna, and then the financial directors who followed him. Parmalat's bonds were rapidly downgraded and the Italian stock exchange suspended trading in Parmalat shares. Tanzi fled to South America, but returned in December 2004 when he was arrested.

The usual issues followed. Somehow the company and its employees had to be saved. The Italian Government under Prime Minister Silvio Berlusconi was forced to use new legislation to protect jobs. This allowed a corporate "turnaround specialist" (Enrico Bondi) to become administrator. The company was granted insolvency status, in order to return to its core business of milk and juice production. It rapidly emerged that Tanzi and his senior directors had forged documents. Eventually, Calisto Tanzi was arrested. His lawyer stated that Tanzi admitted to diverting more than €800 million over the past decade from the company to his personal accounts.

How was it that a man who seemed so generous was also so greedy? Indeed, Tanzi accumulated a fortune for himself and his family. He enjoyed the power and approval that came his way through his benevolent acts; acts that could be performed because of his wealth. The story has the air of medieval Italian power and patronage in the form of a modern entrepreneur. Magazine *Fast Company*,[4] describes the Parmalat story in terms of an Italian opera with Tanzi and Tonna in flamboyant roles, finally turning on each other; greed eventually turning to betrayal. It is within the scope of tragic vision to see personal weakness and greed at the root of the story so that in December 2003 judge Guido Piffer of Milan, following a preliminary investigation, stated in his report that Tanzi was wholly responsible for the "criminal conduct" that lies at the root of the Parmalat scandal.[5]

Yet, later, a more complex picture emerged. The BBC in December 2004 reported that several multinational banks including the Bank of America knew of Parmalat's financial difficulties. *Time Magazine,* December 2004 reported:

> Public companies have safeguards against such egregious fraud, but in this case they seemed to have failed. "They were doctoring documents in the most amateurish fashion, and yet got away with it for a decade," says Mel Weiss, a leading US class-action lawyer. "The auditors just accepted it willy-nilly." Grant Thornton, Parmalat's primary auditor for most of the 1990s and still auditor to some of its subsidiaries, initially said it too had been duped. But on New Year's Eve, Grant Thornton suspended the head of its Italian member firm and another partner after the two men were arrested as part of the widening investigation.[6]

Why was it that this group of senior managers and the company board allowed the situation to occur? What of the wider net of institutions that knew of the problems? Where were the checks and balances? Where was the close scrutiny of company records? It may well have been that Tanzi allowed personal greed to overtake him in his executive actions, but it seems the corporation sat within a climate where the turning of a blind eye was institutionalised. Beyond the greed of an individual, the institutionalised support of the failing giant multinational was tied in with the broader culture of acquisition represented in the international banking world. We find indications of an overarching acquisitiveness that blinds the banks to a correct assessment of the risks they are taking.

The Nature of Greed

An examination of the nature of greed may be helpful before analysing the Parmalat story in terms of perverse corporate dynamics. To explore greed I will go to its earliest development. This will eventually illuminate the notion of greed in adult and organisational behaviour. In this analysis, greed will be examined through its oral, anal and phallic forms: gluttony, avarice and a lust for power. Each of these forms has links to the others and is driven by unconscious forces.

Infant Greed and the Unconscious

A mother may experience her healthy baby as having a lusty zest for life expressed through enthusiastic feeding. When hungry, the baby sometimes sucks greedily at breast or bottle as if wanting to empty it all at once. A hallmark of greed is the intent to find a supply and take as much as possible; to drain the supply, perhaps driven by the fear that there will be no more. The desire to have it all at once sits with the fantasy that the supply may dry up or be witheld by an even greedier or persecuting presence. In working with young children, Melanie Klein[7] came to understand and theorise what she saw as the psychic and emotional developments behind the infant's relation to feeding and to the breast. She understood the breast as the first "part-object" internalised in the infant psyche. That is, because of the importance and centrality of feeding and handling during feeding, this complex of activities forms the major backdrop or context to the developing infant psyche. The infant comes to feel, and gradually to think about the experience that is in and surrounds feeding and the breast. The breast and the experiences associated to it is incorporated into the developing infant mind where it is linked to primitive and instinctual urges.

Following Freud, Klein sees these urges as both life giving and death seeking: creative and destructive. The infant's experiences of the breast come through the filter of these urges, just as our adult experiences come to us through the filters of our wishes, opinions, values and what are popularly known as mindsets. Life and pleasure forces are associated with the sustaining, comforting, hunger-assuaging properties of milk, the giving of it by mother and associated feelings in the infant. An idea of the good breast is formed. Indeed, the feeding situation can serve many purposes including sustenance, comfort and the driving away of pain and fear. In contrast, death and destructive forces are associated with pain, frustration and attendant anger. The absence of the good breast leaves a feeling of hunger, pain and abandonment. These bad feelings are experienced as persecuting. An image of the bad breast is formed. This is the breast that deprives and even inflicts pain.

In order to handle the mixture of conflicting feelings and experiences, the infant uses a process of "splitting". This means that the developing infant psyche forms two parts, or two internal objects based on its experience—the good (breast) and the bad (breast). Both good and bad breasts are ideas soaked in emotion that become internalised. Or, perhaps a better way of putting this is that they are each an experience that comes to be thought about through its internalisation.

We can understand Klein's formulation through an analogy with foetal physical development. When fertilised, the human egg rapidly divides into many cells and, quite early in the gestation period, different groups of cells specialise in order to potentially become particular organs. Very early on, the cells retain their capacity to become any kind of cell, say, a liver or brain cell. These are the famous stem cells. Later, their specialisation becomes complete and the potential for becoming a different kind of cell is lost. If we take such a view to psychic development (and this should not be confused with accompanying brain development), we might say that the early psyche has the propensity to split and divide in order to accommodate the specialisation needed to process emotional experience. This later includes the processing of conceptual experience as the mind and a capacity for thinking grows. The splitting process, together with accompanying projections of experiences into the split-off parts, becomes a prototypical device for handling unbearable feelings. Understanding and evaluating good and bad experiences are equally important. The internal balance between inner objects that are good and bad, and their relations with one another, are critical to the growing mind.

Kleinians and other object relations theorists talk of the infant "splitting" the developing ego in order to create good and bad objects, as if there is a wilful, albeit unconscious infant who deliberately does this. In physical development, we say the fertilised egg divides into multiple cells. The issue of volition is not present. But, this is where the idea of the unconscious enters. The language of psychoanalysis has grown in the consulting room where child and adult patients examine their own thoughts, feelings and behaviours— through relevant methods such as play, free association, interpretation and reflection. The discovery of unconscious processes by Freud helps to explain the breaks in conscious thought and volition. It names those processes where the individual, by inference, must have had a thought or a feeling or a desire but had not been aware of it. These thoughts, feelings and desires are discovered and uncovered through the work of the analysis. Gaps are filled, but the analytic work is not simply a logical process of filling them. It requires the emotional work by the patient of discovering how the unconscious processes operate in the here and now, which itself requires the working through of powerful unconscious defences against their conscious emergence. Predicated on the idea that the unconscious erupts into conscious life with irrational effects, traditional psychoanalysis is also based on the idea that there is a "method in madness" and that with psychoanalytic work a hidden logic will appear. This hidden logic is within the complexities of an individual mind, which for the object relations theorists is an internal world of psychic objects, part-objects and the complex dynamics inter-relating them.

So, the idea of the unconscious emerged in answer to the complex idea of volition or free will operating outside of awareness. We sometimes feel, think or do things for unconscious reasons. We (our conscious egoic selves) are driven by *something-not-ourselves*. Freud called this the Id where the *something-not-ourselves* comes from instinctual impulses, and called it the Super-ego when the *something-not-ourselves* comes from social and cultural prohibitions, rules and laws. Later psychoanalysts have embellished our understanding of the unconscious. Jacques Lacan,[8] for instance, following the philosopher Hegel (where the *something-not-ourselves* is the *"other"*) extends it in a vision of the unconscious as the "Other" with a capital "O" because he reads it as coming primarily from the world of cultural symbols, prohibitions and laws: a pre-existing social order into which each new infant must enter to become human, and which, when internalised, becomes a central force in the psyche. Melanie Klein sees the unconscious as primarily evidenced in the internal world of fantasy that underpins experience. Her student, Wilfred Bion,[9] refers to the unconscious as the "formless infinite", referring in part to the infinite thoughts possible which have not yet been thought but that can emerge within a culture. For Bion and Lacan, the unconscious is not simply an inner force, but represents a potentiality in the wider group or culture. Certainly in these terms we can understand that unconscious processes occur in groups and organisations.

This brings us back to the idea of volition, an idea critical to our understanding of greed. The infant splitting of the ego may be seen as an unconscious device to protect the good from the bad, to remove it so that good experience is able to be used rather than spoilt (by the bad). The idea here is that when good and bad are close to one another, good may be overwhelmed. In many ways, this splitting is a kind of automatic dividing process, just like the cells, except that volition (will) is regarded as present, even though unconscious. Many other processes proceed from this initial split. As mentioned, for the infant, the bad feelings coming through the lens of the death and aggressive instincts are experienced as coming from a persecuting breast, the first part-object of vital importance. Good feelings are seen as coming from a loving, giving breast. So the object is split as well as the ego. Kleinians speak of severe and violent splitting. This may occur in circumstances where the infant's aggression is extreme either due to an inherently strong aggressive impulse or tendency for splitting (a psychotic process) or to severely frustrating and painful circumstances.

Babies differ in their greediness. This is observable. Whether this is a difference in neediness or a character trait to take more than needed, learned at an early age through experience, can only be (imperfectly) studied in each individual case. And we should distinguish between the desire for an object and pursuit of that desire. Is greed a desirous state in itself or a pattern of reactions and behaviours in response to such desire? In this distinction the question of ethics arises. Greed is popularly seen as something over which individuals should have some control. Greed taken into action is popularly seen as an exemplification of the break-down of self-control.

Development beyond infancy sees the further vicissitudes of greed. Gluttony is a form derived from infant greediness and exaggerates the sensuality of eating and drinking. It may unconsciously represent a need for physical comfort and closeness to the mother, but becomes consciously attached to the sensual activity associated with eating, including the taste and texture of food and the social context of eating including its part in power dynamics and friendship.

Gluttony is an old-fashioned term. In this age of psychology, many modern formulations of ideas about gluttony centre around the eating disorders: obesity, anorexia and bulimia. Obesity is linked to poor eating habits and often to poor self-image and a need to eat for comfort or to dispel depression. Sociologically, it is the wealthy western countries that face problems of obesity due to the plentiful availability of processed food. Yet, ironically, it is often exhibited more in their poorer members who have cheap junk food available to them and increasingly this problem is also found in third world countries where western "fast food" has been introduced. We might hypothesise that it is in the economically depressed segments of western society that obesity is increasingly prominent, although, recently there is also much concern for obesity in children from all backgrounds; with concern about the availability of foods with high sugar and fat content in school canteens. Perhaps obesity is a psychological response to personal depression, and a sociological response to changing family-economies and behavioural patterns and economic depression in the midst of plenty.

Some corporate greed can be understood in this way, as a response to perceived psychological and economic depression. At times, corporate greed seems present in the ever demanding cry for increased profits from shareholders, beyond reasonable steady growth. It is as if there is a fear that the source of plenty may dry up and must be exploited before it is withdrawn. This is supported in reality by knowledge that environmental resources are expendible and that irrevocable pollution of the environment is a real risk. Despite this knowledge many corporations persist in denying their effects on the environment, or, perhaps more to the point, in denying that their behaviour in turn will rebound on them in the future. This blindness follows a greedy, selfish view that they are independent of, and can control, the wider system—a linking of pride with greed. Perverse greed often continues to drive corporate behaviour in acquisitions beyond those necessary for reasonable growth. The dangers are both known and denied. Danger is courted and the fantastic belief in power over death and loss is maintained. This is the psychology of gambling at a corporate level.

The psychologically more serious disorders of anorexia nervosa and bulimia, while superficially linked to issues of poor self-image are more integrally connected to issues of power. The most primitive form of power is the control of bodily functions. In these eating disorders there is often a struggle between the individual and the social system (family or medical system) with regard to eating and body weight or shape. Many power issues become represented in this struggle of life and death. "Gluttony" here is represented in binge eating, or negatively represented in the mixed fascination and abhorrence the anorexic has for food. Similarly, the power struggles for control of functions within corporations may unconsciously represent such struggles over the body corporate. Capital and money become the symbols of such control.

Money and Power

Greed also has an anal form; the "filthy lucre" analysed by Norman O. Brown[10] in terms of the Freudian hypothesis that faeces unconsciously equals money. Brown's argument finds that wealth, created from surplus production and leading to commodification and the social division of labour with its inequities demonstrated by Marx, is based on the desexualisation and negation of anality. This brings the projection of negated anality into culture. As social historian, Brown rejects the idea that economic history is a direct result of the exchange value of money. Prior to its exchange value, money (or the pre-money barter symbols of crops, teeth, beads) first came to have sacred value: orginally given to the gods as surplus and later hoarded as accumulated wealth by the priestly elite and priviledged. Money/faeces thus is the symbol of power in society; rampant consumerism, the expression of infantile polymorphous perverse sexuality. Both are the expression of a wish for immortality and a denial of death.

> What the psychoanalytic paradox is asserting is that "things" which are possessed and accumulated, the property and the universal condensed precipitate of property, money, are in their essential nature excremental . . . the infantile wish which sustains the money complex is for a narcissistically self-contained and self replenishing immortal body.[11]

Money and material goods come to represent a capacity to control the body (at first the anal sphincter) and its death in the face of a seemingly demanding civilisation represented through the parents; the "others" who first require such control. In such a fantasy, money comes to represent the power to buy all that is desired, as if the fires of desire might be quenched through a constant stream of consumer goods. Although, in fact, this stream serves simply to feed the fire. To consume means to be consumed by fire, according to the Oxford dictionary. The buying and consuming is inexorably linked to the exercise of power.

Giddens reminds us that, "today, 'money proper' is independent of the means whereby it is represented, taking the form of pure information lodged as figures in a computer printout".[12] In modernity, the accumulation of wealth is not simply sensual, seen and felt in coffers of gold, or bolts of silk. It shows itself as pure symbol, removed far from the body. Modernity for Giddens is partly identified through the presence of systems that are disembedded from their local context. Globalisation requires this and modern monetary systems are examples of such disembeddedness. "Money in its developed form is thus defined above all in terms of credit and debt and . . . is a means of bracketing time and so of lifting transactions out of a particular milieu of exchange".[13] Such a disembeddedness, while enabling a reaching out beyond the local may, in so doing, also require a denial of the power of the local; perhaps a rejection of the body and its limitations.

The foundation of an abstract disembedded social system is trust, Giddens argues, an emotion on which modern societies rely and on which the modern psyche is predicated.[14] It is a different form of trust than that found in pre-modern cultures, where kinship, community, religion and tradition formed the foundations for local face-to-face trust. Modern trust is evidenced in a reliance on abstract distanced systems of technology and impersonal expertise. This is almost a blind trust, instilled in us by those institutions on which we rely for everything in our everyday lives. And still, when trust is broken in these systems we feel shocked and betrayed because a fundamental connection to our sense of everyday life has been destroyed. When debts are not honoured, the rage evoked can lead to violence. A very primitive sense of injustice is aroused. That the system of "money proper" is an expression of social trust may seem a travesty to those poor who seem mostly to enter that system through debt rather than credit. But, in a wry twist, they *can* count on or trust that others will demand their debts be paid. When corporations betray trust, do not pay their debts despite wringing as much profit as possible from the consumers, and when many suffer due to this, the sense of anger and betrayal is immense.

The contemporaneous presence and absence found in abstract systems of disembeddedness, is most evident in modern monetary systems. The notes and coins in our pockets are but a few grains in the vast sea of computerised credits and debits. Money is present, yet absent. If we take Giddens and Brown together, money becomes both a symbol of trust and a symbol of the negation of the body and death. Together these seem to produce a deified symbol, aiding in denial of the existential angst that Giddens sees as lying within modernity. Contemporary money systems, then, are based on the dynamics of perversion as presented in this book: the dynamics of denial alongside the ambivalence about trust embedded in the relations between accomplices and their instrumental use of others.

Greed may also take expression in a phallic form: the greed for power over others, especially their sexuality and desire. In Chapter 3, the phallic culture of the Wall Street money traders was described. An emphasis was placed first on the adolescent character of this culture as described by Lewis, and later on the more aggressive aspects shown by the LTCM traders in their international deals. The picture of phallic greed may link with that of phallic pride. Phallic pride desires to display before the other, perhaps to triumph over the shame of the other, so the other is forced to concede its superiority. The greed for power is a desire to dominate and control the other. At a whole system level, while a Marxist analysis examines this in terms of capitalism as the domination of the system of production by a limited few, this has changed. Nowadays it is a system where many, through privatisation linked to superannuation and government investment, are no longer simply and unambiguously the owners of labour (and in simple false consciousness), but are also the owners of production and so are insidiously tied in with their own wealth creation and, simultaneously, their own domination.

Each of these forms of greed: gluttony, the relentless desire for riches and material goods and the overwhelming desire for power, are developmental expresssions of greed. Whereas appetite, pecuniary interest and assertion of self are the life-giving expressions of each of these impulses, the normal healthy forms that undergird social life, they are turned towards destructivity by perverse greed. The implication of unconscious volition is present. In the vicissitudes of greed, the passive process of division is not primary and it is here that we, perhaps, part company with the analogy of cell division. For, the human psyche is constituted within a cultural context where responsibility, volition and accountability are key foundations. We must be held to account, if not for the development of our psyche and its desirous states, then for our actions. If greed is part of our instinctive inheritance, then its shape and enactment is learned in a cultural context where self-constraint may also be learned and adopted. Or perhaps, more aptly, where the social forms of appetite, pecuniary interest and assertion of self are limited and contained.

Generosity

The impulse to share and be generous can be regarded as the opposite of, yet closely connected to, greed. Klein sees its development as a response to the growing infant's capacity to see mother as a whole person rather than split into good and bad breast. Generosity is associated with a recognition and love of the other, feelings of guilt about destructive impulses towards the other, and a desire to repair past aggressive projections and splitting. A classic sign of peace and reconciliation is found in the communal meal or "breaking/taking of bread together"; the giving and accepting of food. The words companion and company are derived from the Latin roots *"com"* (meaning, *with*) and *"panis"* (meaning, *bread*). It means to draw sustenance with another. Generosity is a building block for relationship with others.

Generosity may be regarded as part of the wellspring of creativity; an impulse to create and give, inwardly to the self and outwardly to others. Generosity towards self helps in the building of confidence and ameliorates harsh self-judgements. This forms a basis for generosity towards others and a desire to share pleasures. Although the Kleinians focus on generosity in the form of reparation, infant development also shows signs of generosity in non-reparative, directly connective forms. It can be seen as part of the infant's openness to experience and willingness to develop trusting relationships.[15]

Some of our most famous characters in history are marked out by their capacity to give of themselves to others, despite, seemingly, great costs to themselves. Yet, the reward is in enrichment to self and is immeasurable in terms of spirit. Of course, all behaviour, including charitable behaviour is the result of mixed motives, conscious and unconscious impulses and learned character. None-theless, generosity is part of the impulse to generativity, charity and social enterprise.[16]

The analysis of the (sin) of avarice and the (virtue) of generosity seem to be two sides of a coin, two expressions of an impulse in the relation of self to other. Freudian analysis of the sexualisation of greed in oral, anal and phallic stages traces its development in the individual body. Kleinian analysis considers the internal objects formed throughout this development, with a focus on the development of psychological defences against painful impulses and experiences.

The thoughts, feelings and actions surrounding guilt and repara-tion, generosity, and recognition and love of others, unlike greed, are readily seen as linked to conscious volition. Such impulses are regarded within religious thinking as virtues to be achieved through a dedicated pursuit. They are taught in schools as part of community values and lauded in the community as an underpinning of voluntary and charitable work. They are not normally regarded as attitudes that we slip into unknowingly and unconsciously. Unconscious volition seems to sit more comfortably with the devil than the saints; more with the deadly sins than the virtues. This is another aspect of volition and intent; greed as desire is shameful and hidden.

Greed and the Organisation

At the beginning of this chapter I noted that as a community we often regard corporate corruption as due to the conscious desires of greedy executives and board members. As a contrast, in Chapter 1, I explained how unconscious perverse dynamics pervade many aspects of our society and its institutions, including corporations and organisations. I said that systems could "turn a blind eye" as a whole, not recognising the blind spots and not experiencing the perversity in individual character but experiencing it in systemic roles with their associated thoughts and feelings. These are feelings that are *in* the person but not *of* the person: they are *of* the role and the system.[17] It may be useful to think of the greediness or generosity of various organisational players as "released" or enabled through particular social and political forces and dynamics at play. The emotions are released *from* the system and back *into* the system, much as adrenalin may be released in the body, to pervade and influence muscular reactions which, in turn, stimulate the production of more adrenalin.

Earlier it was seen that splitting was a device to create structures for dealing with unbearable feelings so that thinking might occur. Different thoughts and feelings can be "held" in different structures, perhaps to be re-integrated in new ways at a later time. Division of labour in an organisation can be understood in much the same way. Different parts of the organisation not only execute different tasks, but they also "hold" different thoughts and feelings on behalf of the organisation.[18] We can think also of power structures as divisions where different thoughts and feelings are held. Marx[19] demonstrated this well in his analysis of power relations surrounding ownership of the means of production; when division of labour serves the unconscious task of creating dominating and dominated sub-groups.

Of course, to argue in this way brings us head on, once again, with the sticky issue of personal volition. Who causes what? The individual or the social conditions? Where is accountability in the group? In the systemic approach given here causes and effects are interwoven such that causality is never linear but circular, complex, perhaps, chaotic. Yet, even in the sophisticated answers to the conundrum of accountability such as this, we are left with the issue of personal responsibility. How is this dealt with in organisations? And where do the structures developed to deal with it, fall down?

From an examination of recent corporate disasters and the responses of the media, such as the Parmalat story, we can see how corporate greed is understood socially. A popular picture is first painted of the greedy executive or group of executives who dupe others with full personal intent. This view might be translated as: "*personal greed gets the better of them*". Alongside this is a picture of the seemingly duped auditors and bankers who on closer examination have failed in their duty, with due diligence to examine the transactions in which they have engaged. This view might be translated as: "*they just didn't know scenario.*" Later the law has its task of teasing out the accountabilities and responsibilities of individuals and judges their personal culpability; their intents and complicities. The media then give us a feast and blow-by-blow account of how all this proceeds.

In this way, most of our common language for understanding greed in organisations is directed towards the conscious intent of the players. But, on further examination, and with the "as if" (an organisation could be seen as a person) stance taken in this book, other impressions come into view. Greed may blind the whole organisational system and move beyond to other broader system players, enrolling them as accomplices. Hence, perverse greed distorts reason and undermines reasonable risk assessment. Such a wide system effect can be perceived in stock market behaviours as well as corporations.

David Tuckett argues that greed within the stock market creates a belief in a fantasmic object.[20] An infantile fantasy comes to dominate. It centres around the (unconscious) fantasmic object that can bring about great wealth with little effort; the fairy tale goose that lays the golden egg. He analyses the dot com bubble of the late twentieth century in terms of this fantasmic object. At that time, market players believed that the internet began a powerful social change that would transform the nature of consumerism beyond imagination. Companies associated with this fantasmic object became over-idealised. Speculation in the dot com companies accelerated and share prices rose to absurd heights. The perverse nature of this process was demonstrated in market players' refusal to heed warnings put out by some analysts, indeed by many market and financial authorities themselves going outside the normal company assessments and accepting high valuations on companies with few or even no business plans. As Tuckett says, the data was thin, yet belief in the possibilities high. A blind eye was turned to what was usually regarded as prudent and hopes were lodged in the belief of a "new economy" where new rules prevailed.

Eventually, the bubble burst. The unrealistic, greedy dreams of the players came to naught. Stock prices crashed and players were left with their pockets empty and their psyches shamed.

Perverse Greed at Parmalat

So, now this case of greed at Parmalat should be examined in terms of the indicators of perversity at an organisational level that have been presented and used in earlier chapters.

First, there is the issue of narcissistic advantage at the expense of a more general good. We can understand some of this story through understanding Italian village or small town culture where the authority of the Catholic Church as director of conscience has a strong hold. The praise given to Tanzi by Monsignor Grisenti was praise from the highest authority. Tanzi was able to act as the benevolent lord. His and his family's place within the society was secure as were the places of other senior Parmalat directors. Greed and generosity were two sides of the same coin; pride fuelled the greed. The indications here, then, are that a social context existed where generosity came not simply to disguise a narcissistic impulse, but was in fact a major vehicle for the expression of narcissism. One could say it was a perverse generosity. This is not to say that the general culture, including the Church, condoned the fraud. The shock there was as great as it was to the wider world. But the socio-emotional conditions were there for its possibility. In this case, the narcissistic gain through generous acts was bought at the expense of others.

Second, is the denial implicit in this. At the conscious level, fraud was of course denied and covered. But at an unconscious level there was a trick going on. Psychologically speaking, the good generous breast hides the bad devious breast. At the individual level, did Tanzi fool himself? Did he believe that his acts of generosity atoned for his misconduct, or was it all a clever disguise?

> The delay in detecting the fraud can be attributed partly to Italy's notoriously weak financial regulators. But many Italians were reluctant to suspect someone of Tanzi's reputation. "Calisto has a profound Christian faith," muses Monsignor Grisenti, who has known him since the late 1960s. But, if involved in this scandal, "somewhere he must have developed a double person-ality." Others close to Tanzi also describe him as "aggressive," "ambitious," "a born risk taker." "He was always looking ahead to the next thing," says a prominent Parma business leader and Tanzi friend.[21]

At the organisational level, the denial was in the form of blindness despite the warnings. Greed seems to have linked the system players in a fantasy of being good. Tanzi as an individual played the good community man. The corporation played the good and wise company.

Linked to this is the third point. The fraud could not have continued as long as it did without the lax vigilance of other authorities, namely, the banks and the auditors who acted as unconscious accomplices. In this case I examine the corporate sin of greed, but here it is supported by the corporate sin of laxity (sloth— see Chapter 6). Greed in the wider system led to a blindness about risk, this led to a laziness about attending to possible dangers. In 2004 the world press was reporting how Parmalat was vigorously engaged in sueing these bodies following Tanzi's disclosures.

Head of Monte Parma savings bank arrested, reports that investigation spreading to international banks.[22]

Tanzi Talks: Italian papers are reporting the Parmalat founder Calisto Tanzi has given prosecutors list of names of politicians and bankers "at the highest level" who provided "safety net", access to public funds.[23]

Parmalat Bankrupt global dairy firm has issued suits in NY against Citigroup, Deloitte & Touche and Grant Thornton, claiming $8b.[24]

The suits go on, the firm has sued 45 banks suspected of continuing to lend when they knew of financial problems.[25]

I can't comment on the idea of instrumental relations (the fourth indicator of possible perverse practice) at the company level. Perhaps the internal culture of Parmalat was "good enough" in the sense that workers were not exploited. I don't have the evidence to know. However, in the world of multinational companies, the decision makers at the top are so far removed from those engaged in the day-to-day work that to imagine relations were anything but instrumental is difficult. Certainly the vast amounts embezzled indicate that the directors saw the dairy corporation primarily as a cash cow.

Finally, the idea that perversion begets perversion appears present. A small amount embezzeled and undiscovered allowed a boundary to be broken. After that first indiscretion came many others. Abusive cycles are, indeed, hard to break. Corruption breeds corruption because of the complicity of the accomplices and their subsequent denial and self-deception. Bound in with this was the moral self-deception of Tanzi the bountiful benefactor. In Tanzi greed and generosity seemingly sat side by side and it is difficult to know which fed the other.

So, in this case, the nature of perverse dynamics becomes evident. A whole systemic process is involved. Tanzi was in a position of power to exploit the dynamic; perhaps to enact it as if it were just second nature. Critically, the financial institutions were complicit. All in the perverse system withdrew at a critical point from their agreed task roles which then became corrupted.[26]

Notes

1. Gettler, L. (2005). *Organisations Behaving Badly: A Greek tragedy of corporate pathology*. Queensland: Wiley.
2. Levine, D. (2005). "The Corrupt Organisation". *Human Relations*, 58 (6): 723–40.
3. *Time Magazine*, January 2004.
4. *Fast Company*, March 2004
5. OpenFacts, the Open Source Knowledge Database.
6. *Time Magazine*, December 2004.
7. Klein, M. (1957). "Envy and Gratitude". In: *Envy and Gratitude and Other Works 1946–1963*. NY: Dell Publishing Co.; and Klein, M. (1975). *Envy and Gratitude and Other Works 1946–1963*. NY: Dell Publishing Co.
8. Lacan, J. (1977). *Ecrits*. London: Tavistock Publications.
9. Gordon Lawrence in his (1998) paper "Won from the Void and Formless Infinite". In: W.G. Lawrence (ed.) *Social Dreaming @ Work*. London: Karnac Books, refers to this idea of Bion's in his (Bion's) *Brazilian Lectures (1975)*. London: Karnac Books, 1990.
10. Brown, N.O. (1959). *Life Against Death: The psychoanalytic meaning of history*. Middletown, CT: Wesleyan University Press.
11. Ibid., pp. 292–3.
12. Giddens, A. (1990). *The Consequences of Modernity*. Oxford: Blackwell, 1991, p. 25.
13. Ibid., p. 24.
14. Both Erik Erikson and Donald Winnicott stress the importance of the development of trust. Erikson, E.H. (1950). *Childhood and Society*. London and NY: W.W. Norton; Winnicott, D.W. (1958). *Collected Papers: Through paediatrics to psychoanalysis*. London: Tavistock Publications.

15. Hamilton, V. (1982). *Narcissus and Oedipus: The children of psychoanalysis.* London, Boston: Routledge and Kegan Paul.
16. Gillin, L. and Long, S. (2004). "Integration of Psycho-Social Theory". Paper given at Conference of Small Enterprise Association of Australia and New Zealand, Brisbane, Australia.
17. David Armstrong uses this phrase *"in* but not *of* the person". See, for example, Armstrong, D. (1995). "The Analytic Object in Organisational Work". Paper delivered at the *Symposium of the International Society for the Psychoanalytic Study of Organisations.* London, July, 1995.
18. Long, S. (2000a). "Competition and co-operation: two sides of the same coin". In: R. Wiesner and B. Millet (eds) *Current Issues in Organizational Behaviour.* Queensland: Jacaranda Wiley.
19. Marx, K. (1906). *Capital: A critique of political economy.* In 3 volumes edited by Fredrick Engles. Chicago, IL: Charles H. Kerr and Co.
20. Tuckett, D. (2006). Paper delivered at Melbourne University.
21. *Time Magazine,* January 2004.
22. BBC, 20.01.04.
23. *Telegraph,* 30.01.04.
24. BBC, 20.10.04.
25. BBC, 17.12.04.
26. Chapman, J. (1999). "Hatred and Corruption of Task". *Socio-Analysis,* 1 (2): 127–50.

CHAPTER FIVE

Envy

As has been stressed in previous chapters, perversion is exemplified by a series of indicators: individual pleasure at the expense of mutuality (or, in broad social terms, a more general good); the paradoxical dynamic of denial of reality, where what is known is at the same time not known (or, as an example in corporate terms, disparate and contradictory public and private images exist in parallel); the use of accomplices in an instrumental social relation; and the self perpetuation or closedness of the perverse dynamic. The perverse culture makes itself evident in many business organisations and contemporary corporations. What of other forms of organisation?

This chapter will examine the perverse dynamic and its relation to the different structural forms of hierarchy and association. While hierarchy is the form taken by organisations to delineate and structure accountability[1] it institutes dependency and stimulates envy. Competition as well as subservience is naturally stimulated by the accompanying counterdependent rivalrous climate of "superiors" and "inferiors", "bosses" and "subordinates", where the imperative is to climb the promotions ladder and supercede one's previous masters. Many times, the competitive climate leads to envy. Take the example where a person is promoted and previous peers are now accountable to that person. Envy surrounding the promotion must be contended with and may cause problems. Association, by contrast is a form of equalisation—democratic but structured as a defence against envious rivalry. Its danger is that it may render difference as equivalence and hence stymie creativity.

Most organisations combine hierarchical with associative structures—a major differential being that between the hierarchical company management–worker structure and its associatively structured board. The hierarchy stimulates envy, while the association defends against it. Together they provide an interesting partnership. Hierarchy, with its vertical parent–child-like authority structures, and association, with its horizontal sibling-like authority structures, might be seen together as a social "envy management" machine, creating envy in one place and repressing it in another.[2] This social envy management machine is held in fine balance. The psychodynamics and psychological economics of envy, as they are generated and defended against through these different social structures, may be moderated or they may become corrupted or unconsciously perverse. This chapter will explore these dynamics, especially as they relate to professional associations.

Destructivity and Domination

To understand the perversity of envy requires a deeper exploration of the paradoxical nature of destructivity and creativity in life, sexuality and perversion. I will do this in the first part of this chapter, leaving you, the reader, to make links to your own experience. I will then explore the dynamics of envy and their place in professional associations.

Perversion is at its very basis linked to destructivity and domination. This is not due simply to its roots in narcissism with its constant self-reference. Narcissism is not necessarily destructive. It can quite adequately serve the life instincts. Perversity depends upon the extent of narcissism present and how this, in turn, broadly structures perverse social relations through instrumentality. The modern age has compelled us to "be yourself"; an individuality heir to nineteenth-century romanticism and later, ironically, popularly understood Freudian psychoanalysis. We live by the notion of self-expression as therapeutic. In fact, this has a longer history than psychoanalysis. Lasch, following Jung, argues that such a view reaches back to Christ whose essential message, Lasch claims, was that we should truly lead our lives in all their implications as he did;

the imperative being: growth through self-knowledge.[3] Whatever the origins of the idea of expressive individualism and a healthy narcissism, it is its perversion into a self-serving use and abuse of others that leads to social destructivity.

The destructivity of perversion lies with the joining of instrumentality and domination to narcissism. As argued in Chapter 2, the "other" is experienced instrumentally, becoming a subject(ed) object to be *used* rather than a subject to be *known*. Hence, the inherent subjectivity of the other is actively attacked in the perverse relation. But, it is not just the other who is attacked. As Hegel demonstrated, the subjectivity of self is also in danger of being destroyed.[4]

Hegel's description of the Master/Slave dynamic examines how, in relations of domination, the Master paradoxically requires the recognition of the Slave to maintain his power. If the Slave is nothing, then the Master's power cannot be recognised. The Slave, seemingly by definition having no will, must yet have will enough if the Master is to keep himself as Master. Something of the other's subjectivity must be kept alive. Instrumentality needs to both promote and subjugate the subjectivity of other. Because if the Slave as "other" disappears, the Master, left alone and unrecognised, also disappears. In a sense, each is the extension of the other, insofar as each is interdependent with the other. The Slave benefits from the relationship, even if this is by no means comparable to the power gained by the Master and is locked into his or her dependency. The perverse relation is both destructive and creative. It must keep alive that which it wishes to destroy. In this, it is a mystery.[5] The indestructible otherness of the Slave brings hope that the relation can move from the perverse parasitical position towards creative social change.

Sado-masochistic perversity is based on such a paradox. Sado-masochistic relations that recognise at some level the interplay of mutual, rather than simply one-sided pleasure, ultimately indicate the paradox of the Master/Slave. The other is used to achieve pleasure. Pleasure is gained *through*, not *with* the other. This is the complex face of perversity, that while linked to the death instincts in its cyclical repetition, its destructivity is also linked to sexual excitation and built around what Lacan calls jouissance.[6] Jouissance is that pleasure/pain derived through satisfaction of what one is unconsciously driven to do; that which is at the core of character.[7] It is the excitation that may be pleasurable, but may incite horror or disgust[8] because pleasure is a complex response to both desire and conscience. We are not always pleased by what we want. A task of the mature personality is to link conscious desire (what one wants or yearns for) to what one is unconsciously driven to do, such that jouissance can be achieved in at least partially socially responsible ways. Freud gives the example of sublimation, where drive, desire and pleasure are joined in creative achievements. Creativity can be seen as incorporating the transgressive aspects of perversion holding or containing the destructivity, while simultaneously expressing its existence.[9]

Psychoanalysis argues that human sexuality develops from the polymorphous perverse pleasure of infancy through to the socialised form of genital sexuality.[10] Although infantile forms are retained in adulthood, these are subsumed under more adult expressions of sexuality and integrated into foreplay or private fantasy. This development is primarily achieved in the early years within the family or kinship group with its biological and social hierarchies. For society, suppression is a necessary aspect because socialisation implies a willingness to give up some individual pleasures to meet group expectations and needs. Also, movement away from incest towards marriage outside the family group is required. Hence, social, economic and political interests are furthered through the taming of polymorphous sexuality and oedipal impulses. But, rather than simple suppression, these political ends are achieved through psychological means—repression. In simple terms, the individual suppresses him or herself and through repression, does not know this.

However, jouissance is achieved in a sexuality that is not repressed or evaded—"the little death" of orgasm, where self fades. Normal sexual pleasure comes close to perverse pleasure on this dimension. The lover is able to gain his or her jouissance through the other, perhaps through desire fired by a fragment, a part-object, a look, a body part, the sound of a voice, the twist of a head. In this way, the lover is achieving pleasure through the other "as if" perverse. This partially explains the (social) linking of sexuality with shame and guilt. The lover recognises and owns that at some level, both s/he and the other are rendered slave to desire through being rendered as part-objects. Perversity and sexuality lie close together, each with the seeds of creativity and destructivity within.

It is difficult to talk about so-called "normal" sexuality from a scientific stance, without recognising the influence of social and moral implications. Normality is not so much a scientific as a cultural concept. What is normal for one may not seem normal for another. What is "average" cannot encompass the range of human sexual expression. Psychoanalytic explanations have often joined with moralistic viewpoints. Like other sciences, it is part of the moral universe. So how can perverse and non-perverse sexuality be distinguished? It is generally agreed that where love-making is within an interpersonal relation of mutual recognition and this within the symbolic set of relations that make up our co-dependent social roles, its perversity is tempered. This occurs within the social symbolic container of relationship—even transitory relationship. The fading from subjectivity during sexual passion is held or contained within mutual social relatedness and restored in social relatedness. The erotic relation is a deep form of mutual recognition.[11]

Kernberg describes mature sexuality:

From a psychoanalytic viewpoint, normality implies the integration of early, pregenital fantasy and activity, the capacity to achieve sexual excitement and orgasm in intercourse and the capacity to integrate into sexual fantasy, play and activity, aspects of the sadistic, masochistic, voyeuristic, exhibitionistic and fetishistic components of polymorphous, perverse infantile sexuality. In fact, from a psychoanalytic viewpoint, the integration of polymorphous perverse infantile sexuality into a tender and loving relationship within which mutual gratification and idealization reinforce and are reinforced by the sexual encounter, reflects an optimum of psychological freedom and normality.[12]

In many senses, some degree of perversity is "normal". Lacan refers to socially required subjugation as "symbolic castration".[13] In being subject to culture, primarily through language, one is subject to the Symbolic field. This is what Lacan also terms the big "Other". In this process of symbolic castration, much jouissance is given over to repression and the Other. The subjection (symbolic castration) that creates subjectivity, forever divides the human subject from his or her primal nature, because the world of symbols can only represent reality, not replicate it. Hence, the subject in the world of symbolisation, language and all that they imply, will lack something. This is the part that cannot be represented; the part that can never become part of the symbolic world wherein we mostly live. This part lies within the register of the Real. Experience registered in the Real cannot be represented in our normal everyday world. It is ineffable. So, in one sense, for the civilised person, jouissance is personally lost and is lacking. In another sense, it becomes part of the psycho-dynamics of community—linked into language and culture as well as into our sense of the ineffable or unknown, with all its awesome, wonder-full and terrifying characteristics.

In the perverse position, symbolic castration has failed. The perverse part of the personality is not subject to the greater good. The perverse process does not repress, evade or deny jouissance. But equally, in the perverse relation (which is a longer- term interpersonal or even social structure) jouissance is totally uncontained. It is incapable of sublimation, which requires subjugation to the wider social good, if we consider the establishment of culture as a wider social good. Jouissance is experienced without containment. Reality is held with ambivalence and relations of instrumentality dominate. Following Lacan's analysis, in perversion no lack is felt. Omnipotence seems supreme. The positive is that the individual feels free from domination, especially the self-imposed domination of his own cultural creations. The negative is that this freedom has the price of the absence of real others who can provide love and recognition. In many senses it is a position of freedom from illusion. But, illusion is also the very centre of our creative existence.

Nonetheless, despite its freedom, the perverse position is needy in its narcissistic roots. Because the relation to reality is complex and an "other" is required, Hegel's Master's dilemma is present. The boundary between the perverse and the normal is a shifting territory between omnipotence and neediness; dominance and mutuality.

Envy

The destructivity of the perverse position is clearly seen in envy. Envy is often regarded as the most destructive of emotions and one in which perverse pleasure/jouissance is intense. Whereas hate may wish to destroy the other, envy wishes to spoil and destroy the very quality that is envied. This may not be recognised and the wish to spoil may be unconscious; hidden beneath a surface longing.[14] In contradistinction to admiration, envy does not simply recognise the desirable in someone else. "Envy is the angry feeling that another person possesses and enjoys something that is desirable—the envious impulse being to take it away or to spoil it."[15] Envy is malicious. It implies the statement "If I can't have it, no one can!" This is exemplified in Shakespeare's Othello. Othello is a successful general, but also proud and jealous. He is a Moor within white society, who through his power and success marries the young and beautiful Desdemona. His underlying insecurity leads him to doubt her fidelity. Iago is a lowly ensign who is deeply envious of his master, Othello. He manages through deception to gain Othello's favour and promotion and from this position to convince Othello of Desdemona's infidelity. Driven by jealousy, Othello kills Desdemona.

Traditional interpretations of the play see Othello as the man with a tragic flaw of pride linked to jealousy. The story is one where a proud and jealous man becomes the prey of a perverse and envious destructive force, perhaps ultimately from within himself.[16] Whereas anger, jealousy and hatred may have sought to directly destroy Othello, envy, in a cloak of friendship destroys that which he desires. Iago is the vehicle who, through his envy, brings destruction to them all. Stein examines the role of Iago in terms of its social, organisational and intrapsychic dynamics, arguing that at the intrapersonal level Iago represents an inner struggle that the leader has with his own envious feelings.[17]

Although envy is a normal part of the emotional make-up of human beings and may stimulate a creative wish to emulate, when acted upon it is an emotion that is most clearly perverse. It is an emotion that in expression destroys self as well as other. The phrase "cut off your nose to spite your face" comes to mind. This self-destructive force has been recognised throughout history. At Hesset, Suffolk in the UK is a medieval painting of the seven deadly sins. Each of the sins, depicted in human form, stands on a different branch of a tree. "Envy's face is gaunt, almost cadaverous, and the emphasis is on the self-consuming nature of the sin."[18] Similarly, Shakespeare's envious Cassius is depicted as having a "lean and hungry look" as if the emotion is eating away at him.

What is at stake in envy is not so much possession of the object of desire, that impulse lies more at the basis of jealousy, another linked and often destructive emotion. In envy, we essentially want what we know the other wants or possesses; we are constantly in the thrall of the desire of the other. This is easily seen in young children for whom the most attractive toy is inevitably the one that another child holds—a parable for adult envy. Moreover, it is a moot point as to whether rivalry grows because the other *has* what we want, or, desire for a possession grows because it *is a rival* who holds it.[19] Although, Lacan's idea (namely, that desire is the desire of the other)[20] means that our very nature is determined by the powerful desire of the other, it is argued here that what is at stake in envy is the growth of rivalry and malice towards the powerful and envied other. This rivalrous malice brings with it a destructive jouissance.

Envy holds an ambivalent stance towards the object, having simultaneously both the desire to possess it and the desire to destroy it in order to spite the (powerful) other. This powerful other is the one who possesses the desired object, or, more correctly, who embodies the desired characteristic, because the other is primarily envied for something he or she *is*, not simply what he or she has. Othello was not envied by Iago simply for his possession of Desdemond, but for who he was—a powerful general who, despite being the alien other (a Moor) enjoyed the best rewards of white society. For the envious, the other contains all that is desirable. If envy were simply desire for the objects possessed by the other, simple imitation or theft would prove solutions. But they do not. The envious wants power over the other; to take out from the other all that is desirable and to destroy it. This aspect of envy, that is, the desire to destroy what is envied in the other, is ultimately an attack on goodness[21] which also includes good authority, that capacity of the other to represent, embody or act on behalf of the whole. Envy would not have the other represent anything. Inherent in this position is the wish to destroy the greater good. Herein lies its perversity in the desire to destroy the common good and, yet, also in its need to both sustain and attack the subjectivity of the other; to both have and deny the subjectivity of the other in instrumental use where the very being of the other sustains the envy.

When envy is fully enacted, envious possession is through destruction and what is finally possessed is damaged or dead. This is the perverse dynamic underlying the extreme destructiveness of sexual abuse, rape and even necrophilia. Chasseguet-Smirgel describes a Czechoslovakian film *The Corpse Incinerator* whose central character is a necrophile who "disguises the anal-sadistic character of his occupation (he works in a crematorium) by idealizing it".[22] He describes death as beautiful and cremation as allowing the soul to escape the body. But this is an intellectualised cover for his perversion that eventually leads to murder and to his work for the Nazis at a death camp. The ideology of Nazism with its wish for a "pure" race allowed him and his perversion to become part of the group.

Such perversions may seem far away from the everyday little pangs of envy that besiege us in a narcissistic and consumerist society. But, the dynamics of envy are constantly at play in organisations where competition is a fundamental reality and organisational players view themselves in the light of the successes and failures of others. How might such dynamics be expressed in organisations and when do they eventuate in destructive behaviours? Alternatively, when might they be transformed into creative processes?

Professional Associations

Envy will be explored here through looking at its functioning in professional associations. Envy is known to grow in situations of dependency.[23] In many ways, although sad to admit, the greatest envy is generated among those closest to one another and is especially fuelled in competitive situations which transform to rivalry. The archetypal story of Cain and Abel, a story of sibling rivalry, is testament to this. Similarly, many family businesses run into problems due to both jealousy and envy amongst family members. Stein analyses the Gucci family business in these terms.[24] If morality consists not so much in doing active good as in exercising restraint and doing least harm, then the restraint of envy within close association should surely be high on the list of ethical virtues. Through exploring associations, some idea of the presence and restraint of envy can be discerned.

As a form of organisation, the association appears to be quite different from the corporate form previously discussed, and to bureaucratic hierarchies. Yet, the association form lies at the heart of the corporation, hence, understanding its dynamics is critical. The association is at the heart of the corporation because it is the organisational form of the Board of Directors. The board's nature as an association must be examined because of the potential influence it has. Whereas the CEO, the senior managers and so on down the authority line do the operational work of the corporation, it is the board that has the major responsibility for direction—even when in practice that too is delegated to management.

Corporate accountability hierarchies and associations are structurally different.[25] Bureaucracies are accountability hierarchies with varying degrees of purity. They consist formally as a structure of layers where, at each level, the higher layer of personnel has authority over the lower layer and the lower layer is accountable to the higher layer. Much traditional government-owned enterprise and its heirs have such a bureaucratic structure. And, in general, corporations are accountability hierarchies where workers are eventually accountable to a senior management which, in turn, is accountable to a board representing the shareholders, or to a family or owner in the case of a private business.

The hierarchy lends itself to the master/slave dynamic because of the way that authorised power is distributed. There are managers and subordinates. Checks and balances hold or contain this dynamic and modify its expression. For example, in organisational hierarchies, good authority represents the *agreed collective task*—a social contract rather than the personal interests and personal power of the holder of the authorised role. This agreement helps to modify the inherent instrumentality of the hierarchy. Of course, power may be distributed in ways that counterbalance the formal authority structure through the informal or shadow system.[26] Indeed, workers at all levels may hold power, for instance, due to their expertise, personal attributes or their ability to represent the interests of others. Many forms of distributed leadership may be present and teams may appear to function in non-hierarchical ways. Nonetheless, the master/slave structure of the hierarchy is basic.

An association, by contrast, is a group of "equals". The structure is not layered with accountabilities but each member is accountable to all the others and to the whole. Each directly represents the whole as well as his or her own position. But "equals" is not quite the right word. Political equality does not mean that all members have equal talents or equal desires. It means all have equal rights to representation within the political system. A better way to express the socio-political nature of the association might be to see the structure as one of commonality rather than equality.

What is this political system in the organisation or association? A distinction can be drawn here between task and political systems within the organisation. Although social psychology has long been familiar with the distinctions made between the task and sentient systems in an organisation; its work and social systems, if you like, there are, beyond this simple distinction, multiple systems of, for example, task, power, emotions, social, socio-technical, financial and intellectual (to name some prominent systems). Each system is related to the others but acts in quasi-independent ways. Each has relative autonomy and, this point is critical, each has roles available for members to take up. Often members take up or are offered roles in different systems that bring about internal and/or external conflict.[27] The political system involves the distribution and use of power and authority in the organisation, whether it is an accountability hierarchy or association.

Now, if hierarchy lends itself to the perverse master/slave dynamic, to what does association lend itself? The immediate answer to this question would appear to be democracy. "Democracy means minimally, equality."[28] Democracy is an alternative political organisation or system to the master/slave system within an enterprise or group. However, in democracy, group members are assumed to be equals where equality refers to the distribution of power and influence; or perhaps more correctly in practice, and as indicated above, to the distribution of the right to have one's views represented. But, although representation comes easily to those with power and influence, many so-called democracies go no further than to include these in their decision-making apparatus leaving others dispossessed.[29] Experience teaches that true democracy is hard won and subject to corruption if not guarded. A truer democracy will go beyond simply representing the voices of those who pressure the authorities to finding ways to also represent the poor and the ignored in society.[30] Democracy implies equality of representation in the whole, and, through this process, a right to a share in the resources of the community. It implies a commonality—linked to community and common-wealth.

While, as previously argued, the master/slave dynamic underpins hierarchy but may be modified, or its more destructive effects ameliorated by the social container of relationship and relatedness between subjectivities, democracy seems directly to represent an organisation of subjectivities where each recognises the other and is able thus to assert influence in the community of the group or organisation. A true democracy should recognise intersubjectivity[31] and interdependence,[32] and manage the fine balance between taking "into account the equality of everyone, justice and equity, and nevertheless take into account and respect the heterogeneous singularity of everyone".[33] This sounds ideal, heroic even. But what does this mean psychodynamically?

Psychodynamic Roots of Democracy

The psychodynamic roots of democracy indicate a less idealistic picture, especially as they are linked to envy. Freud's classic myth of the primal horde sees the primitive patriarch as jealously guarding his role of master and his possession of the females in the tribe.[34] His sons are left to gather together at the fringe of the horde, both physically and socially, much as do the young male wolves in a pack, or the groupings of growing colts in a herd of wild horses. Their envy is stimulated.

In the myth, the anger and envy of the sons leads them to collectively murder the father. Overcome by remorse, however, they mourn. In the process of mourning the individual internalises aspects of the person mourned. So, in the myth, each brother identifies with different aspects of the father's character. Through this story Freud argues that the brotherhood of the sons, their democracy if you like, is dynamically created through the process of their envy, resultant remorse and mourning. A democratic group is thus born from the loss of, and mourning for, the narcissistic individual. The dynamic roots of democracy, the myth argues, lie in the collective good triumphing over the narcissistic—perhaps perverse—individual.

The myth can also be taken as an allegory of individual development where a capacity for interpersonal relationship and societal relatedness grows beyond infantile narcissism. The polymorphous perverse position becomes socialised and transforms into mutual intercourse. Such a development is hoped both for the individual and for the social body.

The development from envy, through remorse, to mourning and identification, traces and offers a pathway of recovery from the destructive effects of envy. But must this cycle of emotions always be expressed, or are there social shortcuts to prevent the perverse destructiveness of envy being played out in full? Schoeck argues that socialism is a form of defence against envy.[35] By forming a political relation where members are equal, envy is bound and contained. This idea of socialism goes beyond the basic political democracy of being represented, to an idea of the equal sharing of resources. The path from political representation to socialism wends its way from equality of representation to such ideas as "from each according to his ability to each according to his need". At a basic level, it is as if envy and its destructive effects might be held at bay by the envied showing that they have nothing to be envied; they share all with all. They have a common good. The offering of sacrifices and gifts to the gods may be understood in this light[36] and both Shoeck and Klein argue that rituals designed to ward off the "evil eye" are linked to defences against envy.[37]

The many forms of democracy, socialism and community that exist bear testimony to a variety of impulses including the pursuit of community and the basic need for communion.[38] And, if we are here to understand aspects of socialism as a social psychological condensation of the longer pathway of envy, remorse, mourning and identification, we must also keep in mind the foundation of love in the equation that brings about remorse and a desire for reparation, in addition to the human propensities for empathy and care involved in identification. Nonetheless, the organisational form of democracy or the impulse to socialism understood as social defences against envy are powerful explanatory notions. Perhaps democracy relies both on the positive human propensities towards social-ism[39] and on defences against envy. Freud was rather cynical.

> If one cannot be the favorite oneself, at all events nobody else shall be the favorite ... What appears later in the shape of Gemeingeist, esprit de corps, "group spirit", etc. . . . does not belie its derivation from what was originally envy. No-one must want to put himself forward, everyone must be the same and have the same. Social justice means that we deny ourselves many things so that others may have to do without them as well, or, what is the same thing, may not be able to ask for them.[40]

What has this to do with the organisational form of association? Following the argument presented, the association as a political structure of "equals" may be understood, roughly speaking, as largely constituted from the more or less sophisticated development of a social defence against envy and its destructive social effects. In this formulation, the defence is an unconscious agreement between the group members to avoid the destructive effects of envious impulses.

Although I have stated that association lies at the centre of many work organisations, corporations and not-for-profit associations because that is the political form of their boards, and that gives good reason for understanding the social dynamics of associations, I will not be discussing boards until Chapter 6. Here the examination will be through professional associations.

Professional Associations

It is not surprising that many analyses of professional associations find in these organisations a history of splits, factions and rivalries.[41] It will be argued here that many of these are the result of the operation of both envy and jealousy as dynamics. But, as with the analysis of emotions presented in other chapters, envy and jealousy here are understood in terms of their manifestation within organisation dynamics.

Professional organisations usually begin when an individual or a small group of professionals take an entrepreneurial stance to form the organisation. These professionals are either respected as authorities in their field or able to draw authorities into supporting and taking a role in the establishment of the association. But, the field itself is often new and becoming established—partly through the development of the association. The founders are able to take up leadership and to gain a membership for the association. While a rational conscious process may be followed and a solid work group may be established,[42] this process can also be understood in terms of the avoidance of a type of "sibling rivalry" or sibling envy. How is this?

Professional associations are formed with the explicit purpose of furthering the interests of their members. This is usually in terms of promoting, developing and regulating the profession; providing members with opportunities for professional development, peer discussions and further education; providing a supportive environment for members to discuss practice issues and opportunities for networking. The promotion, development and regulation of the profession are purportedly done with the collectivity of members in mind, that is, for the greater social good of the community of the profession and its clients. This also shapes the discourse of the profession through regulating its content, theories and practices and, most importantly, accrediting its authorities: giving them powers both within the profession and within the broader society that recognises the profession.

A professional organisation is avowedly established for the professionals' networking, education and furthering of the profession—although improved working with clients may be a desired outcome. However, if we understand the relation with the client as fundamental (it is definitory in the meaning of a profession) and interactions with other professionals as secondary, then the association, as an association of equals, is loosely held insofar as the professional/client relation is supported.[43] A major motive for professionals to associate is in order to preserve their work with clients. Also, if what has been said about the psychodynamics of the association holds, then it is also unconsciously formed to defend members against an outbreak of envy in the profession, particularly envy about skills and capacities that help the professional obtain and work with clients, or to obtain a significant reputation in their field. That is, to become Masters.

The composer Brahms said of a minor contemporary composer, Bruckner, who was enjoying at last some celebrity, that his 7th symphony "had a few not unharmonious melodies scattered throughout an otherwise unremarkable piece . . . not unlike globules of fat in a watery soup".[44] The observance of professional rivalry and envy is nothing new, even amongst those who we might think would never be subject to its seductions. But, there are some circumstances under which these emotions become heightened. For instance, the dynamics surrounding envy often get played out as professional associations develop their own training institutes. Frequently these stay tightly coupled with the association and are unregulated from the outside while being the major source of entry to the profession and the association.

In a study of American psychoanalytic institutes, Kirsner describes how the powerful New York Institute functioned much as a cult rather than a professional institute.[45] Through much of the post World War II period up until the 1990s, a small central clique controlled the institute, primarily through its training function. Power was passed on through a process of selecting candidates primarily willing to uphold the authority of the leaders. The induction into psychoanalysis was conferred on those judged able intuitively to take up the work, rather than through a more open judgement of ability, and at various times nepotism and favouritism was rife. Of his work in this area Kirsner says,

> One might examine how François Roustang's important work on discipleship from Freud to Lacan examined how institutes often make their leaders into the owners of knowledge whom the students owe allegiance to in an unquestioning way. Through didactic analyses where the transferences are entrenched rather than examined, the candidate is cemented into the institute as a disciple . . . In all, group psychology supervenes, the issues of orthodoxy and dissidence seem overwhelming, and questions of power and prestige through control of training are paramount . . . Psychoanalytic institutions are normally organised as guilds which, in my view, are really internally focused cliques. They aim at the perpetuation of their ways of thinking (what they assume to be their body of knowledge that they pass on to their students) and tend to foreclose approaches that challenge their assumptions. They are not part of a wider university culture which, despite its many faults, at least rests on some wider protocols and accountability structures.[46]

Kirsner's inclusion of the notion of guild is interesting. The guild is a precursor of the professional association. While the masters in the guild may share a relationship of equality, brotherhood even, the apprentices are the underlings. In looking at the guild or association we can see two fundamental forms of relationship. The first is the professional or tradesman's relationship with their customer/client. The second is the relationship with the apprentice or trainee. The professional or tradesman needs both of these relationships to ensure the viability and sustainability of their business. It might nowadays be politically incorrect to admit it, and one might need ethically to transform or curtail such a feeling, but the emotion that is generated is one of exclusivity or ownership. One's clients and one's trainees/students/apprentices are jealously guarded. And they are a source of envy from others, as are the resources one has in gaining clients and apprentices. As previously discussed, the envy among the siblings is contained and defended against in the guild/association form. What happens then, when the association collectively takes on a training function? In this case, there is the possibility of envy becoming uncontained and perversely enacted.

Training and Perverse Envy

The argument here is that envy becomes perversely enacted and uncontained when the association moves away from its basic democratic structure to take up professional training that is not independently conducted, or at least regulated. Too often the training process—a hierarchical work organisation, with teachers, authorities and students—becomes subjected to the professional rivalries, envy and jealousies barely contained in the association's democratic structure. Particular theories and practices become vehicles of rivalry and arguments grow around training structures; what is to be included and excluded. Despite the overt wish to promote learning within training candidates, the potential for an envious system is present, where all learning is despised.[47] This can be evidenced in practices concerning training candidates that border on the sadistic.[48]

Training is a major boundary function, that is, it determines who enters the profession. Trainees, not yet members of the profession are not regarded as equals but in many senses as inferior. There is a hierarchy and the master/slave dynamic persists. After graduation and upon becoming a full association member, this hierarchy is symbolically removed for the new member. The association is, after all, an association of equals. Yet, despite this ideology, a hierarchy persists amongst the sibling association members once newly trained members enter. Despite the avowal or assumption of equality, a hidden hierarchy, perhaps based on how long one has been in the profession, whether one has held office in the association, where one is published or works, and so on, is present. Some of the players have more personal power than others. A power hierarchy may be present. Relations of domination are implicit.[49]

This should not blind us to the fundamental basic structure of association. It is the institutionalised political structure (of democracy in association) rather than the interpersonal power structure (of hierarchy) of the group that counts in this distinction. A hereditary kingdom is always a hierarchy; an association always a democracy in these terms, even though each may have either a despotic or benevolent power in charge.

The professional association, like all organisations, has a life history. It begins with the association of equals who employ the defences against envy thus far described. It grows through an extended membership. These, through various regulations, may fit with the existing associative structure. At a later stage, younger members, new to the profession, enter. The hidden hierarchy of differential informal power begins to appear. Envy and rivalry, earlier well contained within the defensive structure, may emerge.

Sometimes, training from within the association will be instituted. The conscious rational reasons are many: to sustain and improve the profession; to allow young/new people to gain training and experience and thus qualify for membership of the profession and the association; to allow more experienced members to share their experience. This training function brings in a new authorised hierarchy. Normally, the defence of equality manages the envy aroused in the hidden (or not so hidden) hierarchy. However, where training becomes the ground upon which professional envy is played out, the defence may waver.

While the fundamental organisational form is of association, hierarchies are present as secondary supportive organisational structures. First, professional association leaders are (most often) elected into their leadership roles and the organisational functioning and management will institute a work hierarchy through its various offices.

Fundamentally, office bearers are elected from the general membership and in this sense are interchangeable through the election process. Institutionalised envy surrounding their authorised power is then both socially created and managed through the knowledge that the social position is temporary. However, second, with the addition of the training process, a new official or authorised hierarchy enters. The propensity for these leaders unconsciously to come to stand as parental authorities is heightened, due to the dependencies established during training. While the authorised hierarchies come into place, the hidden hierarchies gain strength. They support the narcissism of individuals, find accomplices who support non-democratic structures and practices and often create further envy, anger and destructiveness.

In the analysis given, the democratic association operates as a defence against envy instating the members as equals. But this is not enough. Further defences are required because of the heightened envy stimulated through the training process and its resultant transferences.[50] In a perverse twist, democracy becomes a new form of autocracy. The usual group dynamics are present and their effects are increased. The general body of professionals place the leaders as role models—in Freud's terms, they put the leader(s) in the place of the ego ideal where they become idealised.[51] This leadership is not one of "manager" as in an accountability hierarchy, but is one of the leader as a representation of the ideal. As such, this is a form of monarchy or oligarchy. The leader represents the ideal (the values within the ego ideal) and, for each of the members, becomes an internalised authority. This is again reinforced through the transferences generated in the training process. The leaders are able to have this place because they are seen to be *beyond* the general body. They stand in the place of higher authorities—ultimately the place of the parents or of the gods: having a position of vertical authority.[52] The group dynamic then becomes one of underlying dependency with the propensity to generate further envy, but without the democratic defence initially instituted by an association.

In contrast to the leadership, the general body of professionals can be understood as equals insofar as they have equivalence in their training and experience. In Freud's terms they are identified with one another in their egos.[53] Unconsciously, this is the sibling position, where horizontal authority may be predominant.

It is wise for professional associations to place a rational time limit on the holding of leadership positions and to build this into their constitutions. If the original leaders are either instituted as, or become basic assumption leaders, either the group may find it hard to replace them or a political rebellion may occur.[54] For instance, if the leader or leadership group remains in position for many years, and if it seems that no one can succeed them, then the basic assumption of dependency may be in operation. A coup or a major split may be the result because the only way out of the thrall of entrenched dependency is for extreme counter-dependency forces in the group to emerge. Such dependency can occur for many reasons. It may be that the leader(s) carry most of the work, hold most of the power or dominate for other reasons, or the group is fearful of the leaders' authority, or members are unwilling to take up authority. Eventually, the dependency leads to anger. Alternatively, if the leaders are instituted or become fight leaders they may become irrelevant to the group once the object of the fight is achieved. In order to stay in office as leaders, new "causes" may be sought. This would demonstrate the presence of basic assumption fight and may lead to a persistent "fight" attitude that is no longer appropriate. Unconsciously, the group may be acting as if the leaders are generals and the members are troops. Although building in limited role tenure may not change a basic assumption—the group may indeed seek new dependency or fight leaders—it does allow the possibility of moving out of an entrenched position, and especially frees up those individuals who are locked into roles, playing out a frozen position as a result of the group dynamic.

Similarly, it is important for professional associations to avoid conducting non-independent training. There is a need for issues of professional training, ethics and quality to be, at minimum, monitored through independent bodies. Apart from the usual issues of conflict of interest—emotional, attitudinal or pecuniary—this analysis indicates that the normal social defences against envy become weakened when the dynamics surrounding training are enmeshed with other association dynamics.

Bion discovered the basic assumptions in his work with therapy groups.[55] These groups are made up of patients (equals in the eyes of the therapist and the therapeutic group) and therapist (the professional "authority" or at least the "other"). This is close to the structure of associations, namely, (equal) members and a leader in the place of ego-ideal. Members and patients are not accountable to their leaders and therapists, at least not as subordinates are to managers. In fact, it is the other way around. The elected leaders of associations are accountable to their members and the therapist to his patients. While Bion's work on basic assumptions has been taken up in the consideration of work groups within authority hierarchies where members are accountable to managers for their work, and although this use of the theory may well be appropriate because the dynamics of the family are frequently projected into the workplace, it would seem that its application to associations is more closely relevant. In associations, the unconscious form of siblings (equals in ego identification) readily occurs, as has been argued. In face of this, the "work group"—that is, the consciously working, rationally organised and functioning association—has to work against the infantilisation of members, or their transformation into acolytes.

The argument here, then, is that while the accountability hierarchy of the work organisation or corporation must establish a rationally sound work group primarily in the face of the (perverse) master/slave dynamic of domination (and thus avoid the enslavement of workers), the professional association must establish a work group primarily in the face of sibling envy and rivalry dynamics.[56] Failure to do so is the failure to stem perverse envy.

This analysis is important when dealing with the dynamics of company boards, for, in contradistinction to the accountability hierarchy of the work organisation, a board is fundamentally an association. At times, however, board members forget their fundamental status and accountabilites and become dominated by selfish motives, fear or other emotions that lead to perverse practice. Issues surrounding boards will be examined in the next chapter.

Notes

1. Jaques, E. (1989). *Requisite Organization: The CEO's guide to creative structure and leadership.* USA: Carson Hall and Co.
2. The idea of an envy management machine can be compared to the natural/social/psychological production machines described by Deleuze and Guattari, 1984. Even though these authors later described their work as a joke or parody (Ragland-Sullivan, E. (1978). *Jacques Lacan and the Philosophy of Psychoanalysis.* Chicago, IL: University of Illinois Press) the idea of the machine-like nature of some unconsciously driven social processes is valid.
3. Lasch, C. (1979). *The Culture of Narcissism: American life in an age of diminishing expectations.* NY: Norton.
4. Hegel, G.W.F. (1998). *Phenomenology of Spirit.* In: S. Houlgate (ed.) *The Hegel Reader.* Oxford: Blackwell Publishers.

5. Benvenuto, S. (2006). "Perversion and charity: an ethical approach".
    In: D. Nobus and L. Downing (eds) (2006). *Perversion: Psychoanalytic
    perspectives*, pp. 59–78. London: Karnac.
6. Lacan, J. (1977). *Ecrits*. London: Tavistock Publications.
7. Salecl, R. (1998). *(Per)versions of Love and Hate*. London: Verso.
8. Fink, B. (1995). *The Lacanian Subject: Between language and jouissance*.
    Princeton, NJ: Princeton University Press.
9. Chasseguet-Smirgel, J. (1984). *Creativity and Perversion*. London:
    Free Association Books; Pajaczkowska, C. (2000). *Ideas in Psycho-
    analysis: Perversion*. UK: Icon Books.
10. Freud, S. Three Essays on the Theory of Sexuality (1905). In: *Sigmund
    Freud: On Sexuality*. Harmondsworth: Penguin, 1977, pp. 31–169.
11. Benjamin, J. (1995). *Like Subjects, Love Objects: Essays on recognition
    and sexual difference*. New Haven, CT: Yale University Press.
12. Kernberg, O. (2006). "Perversion, perversity and normality:
    diagnostic and therapeutic considerations". In: D. Nobus and
    L. Downing (eds) (2006). *Perversion: Psychoanalytic perspectives*,
    pp. 19–38. London: Karnac, p. 21.
13. Lacan, J. (1977), op. cit.
14. Stein, M. (2000b). "After Eden: Envy and the defences against
    anxiety paradigm". *Human Relations*, 53 (2): 193–212.
15. Klein, M. (1975). *Envy and Gratitude and Other Works 1946–1963*. NY:
    Dell Publishing Co., p. 181.
16. Stein, M. (2005). "The Othello Conundrum: The inner contagion of
    leadership". *Organization Studies*, 26 (9): 1405–19.
17. Stein, M. (2005), op. cit.
18. www.paintedchurch.org/hessds.htm.
19. Girard, R. (1972). *Violence and the Sacred*. Baltimore, MD: Johns
    Hopkins University Press.
20. Lacan, J. (1977), op. cit.
21. Klein, M. (1957), op. cit.
22. Chasseguet-Smirgel, J. (1984), op. cit., p. 55.
23. Klein, M. (1957), op. cit.; Stein, M. (2000b), op. cit.
24. Stein, M. (2005), op. cit.
25. Jaques, E. (1989), op. cit.
26. Stacey, R. (2001). *Complex Responsive Processes in Organizations:
    Learning and knowledge creation*. London and NY: Routledge.
27. Newton, J., Long, S. and Sievers, B. (eds) (2006). *Coaching in Depth:
    The organisational role analysis approach*. London: Karnac.

28. Derrida, J. (1997). Politics and Friendship: A discussion with Jacques Derrida. Center for Modern French Thought, University of Sussex, 1 December 1997.

29. Gordon, M. (2006). "A democracy to come: first the small group and then the world". Unpublished paper.

30. Freire, P. (1970). *Pedogogy of the Oppressed*. London: Penguin Books; Rosenfeld, J.M. and Tardieu, B. (2000). *Artisans of Democracy: How ordinary people, families in extreme poverty, and social institutions become allies to overcome social exclusion*. Maryland, USA: University Press of America.

31. Benjamin, J. (1988). *The Bonds of Love*. NY: Pantheon Books; and (1995). *Like Subjects, Love Objects: Essays on recognition and sexual difference*. New Haven, CT: Yale University Press.

32. Lawrence, W.G. (2000). *Tongued with Fire: Groups in experience*. London: Karnac Books.

33. Derrida, J. (1997), op. cit.

34. Freud, S. (1913). *Totem and Taboo*. London: Routledge and Kegan Paul, 1960.

35. Schoeck, H. (1966). *Envy: A theory of social behaviour*. NY: Harcourt, Brace and World.

36. Slater, P.E. (1966). *Microcosm: Structural, psychological and religious evolution in groups*. NY: John Wiley and Sons.

37. Klein, M. (1957), op. cit.; Schoeck, H. (1966), op. cit.

38. The basic need for community is one of the major concepts in Adlerian theory. Adler, A. (1998). *Social Interest* (revised edition). London: Oneworld Publications.

39. Lawrence, W.G. (2000), op. cit.

40. Chasseguet-Smirgel, J. (1984), op. cit., p. 59; quoting Freud, 1921 (Freud, S. (1921). *Group Psychology and the Analysis of the Ego*. London: Hogarth Press and the Institute of Psychoanalysis (1949) pp. 120–1.)

41. Eisold, K. (1998). "The splitting of the New York Psychoanalytic Society and the construction of psychoanalytic authority". *The International Journal of Psycho-Analysis* (October), 79 (5): 871–85; and Eisold, K. (1994). "The Intolerance of Diversity in Psychoanalytic Institutes". *Journal of Applied Psychoanalysis*, 75: 785–800. Kirsner, D. (2000). *Unfree Associations: Inside psychoanalytic institutes*. NY: Other Press; Fraher, A. (2004). *A History of Group Study and Psychodynamic Organizations*. NY: Free Association Books. Although these studies

are focused on psychoanalytic association, the dynamics are applicable to other professional associations.

42. Bion, W.R. (1961). *Experiences in Groups*. London: Tavistock Publications

43. The professional works primarily in an independent fashion with a client, using their expertise to inform and guide the client's decisions. Although professionals may work as teams and also collaborate on various tasks and work together in large organisations, corporations even, their primary working mode is to pair with the client or group of clients to achieve an outcome. Take an accountant, a lawyer, a teacher, a physician or a psychoanalyst as an example. Bion's ideas of relatedness echo ecological relations described in the biological sciences, these are commensal, parasitic and symbiotic relations (Bion, W.R. (1970). *Attention and Interpretation*. London: Tavistock Publications). It should be remembered that the commensal relation is one of working side by side, while the parasitic relation is perverse, with one party "feeding off" the other to its detriment. The symbiotic relation is one where both parties (perhaps all parties in multi-party relations) gain through the relations developed. So, we can think of the professional–client relation in these terms. The ideal relation is a symbiotic one with professional and client working as a collaborative pair. The perverse relation occurs when the professional "feeds off" their client. Professional associations tend to be commensal, with professionals working side by side, perhaps learning from one another, sometimes collaborating but basically operating independently and gathering together for support. This semi-independence works well to defend against an outbreak of destructive competition, which might otherwise emerge without the containing function of good leadership. Brigid Nossal's unpublished PhD from RMIT University deals with the difficulties of professionals working together. Nossal, B. (2007). *Systems Psychodynamics*.

44. ABC Classic FM Radio, 06.02.07.

45. Kirsner, D. (2000), op. cit.

46. Kirsner, D. (1999). "Life among the analysts". *Free Associations*, 17 (43).

47. Stein, M. (2000b), op. cit.

48. Otto Kernberg has been concerned for many years with issues in psychoanalytic training. See, for example, Kernberg, O. (1996). "Thirty methods to destroy the creativity of psychoanalytic candidates". *International Journal of Psycho-Analysis*, 77 (5): 1031–40.

49. The Group Relations Training field has retained the idea of association, at least in theory, through the practice that among the staff of the group relations training programmes, the leader (conference director) is referred to as "first among equals". At least, this was promoted by the founders of the group relations training method. The training conferences of the Tavistock Institute of Human Relations (and other similar organisations around the world) deal predominantly with learning from experience about issues of authority and leadership. In practice, the conference director is often treated by members (and staff) as a hierarchical leader. This attribution is available for study along with other attributions about authority in the conferences. Group relations associations, however, are open to the dynamics discussed in this chapter, just as are any other associations. See, for example, Fraher, A. (2004), op. cit.

50. Douglas Kirsner (2000, op. cit.) describes how the training function, especially the training analysis, is a central problem in psychoanalytic institutes. He argues that because psychoanalysis is not a science and many psychoanalytic concepts are defined differently in different psychoanalytic schools, psychoanalytic institutes are susceptible to becoming cult-like—just as he finds in his analyses of several US psychoanalytic institutes. Moreover, adding to this susceptibility, the training analysis, he says, confuses the two roles of student and patient, which adds in strong transferential processes, and in the institutes the ability of analysts is often thought about in somewhat magical terms. He argues that training should be separated from the political issues within the institutes and the influence that training analysts have over the careers of the students. I agree with his conclusion, but believe that the issue of the independence of training is relevant to associations beyond psychoanalytic institutes. That psychoanalysis is not a science is not so important. (I won't argue whether or not it is a science at this stage.) Even scientific associations can fall prey to cult-like dynamics. What is important, is that in the training function, the organisational defences against envy are weakened and, subsequently, tendencies for splitting and factionalisation increase.

51. Freud, S. (1921), op. cit.

52. For discussion of vertical and horizontal authority see Long, S. (2006). "This used to be my playground: family/work dynamics". In: A. Mathur (ed.) *Dare to Think the Unthought Known*. Tampere: Aivoairut Publishing, pp. 135–52; and Slater, P. (1966), op. cit.

53. Freud, S. (1921), op. cit.
54. Bion, W.R. (1961), op. cit.
55. Ibid.
56. The post-modern work organisation may blur this distinction somewhat, where structures of semi-autonomous teams, quasi-democratic job design, distributed leadership and networked structures appear to institute a more democratic form rather than the despotic primal horde or master/slave form. We may seem to be experiencing some transformation from the accountability hierarchy to a form closer to the association. However, the distinction holds despite these changes. An analysis in terms of the commodification of society (Marx) helps to make this clearer and is approached in the final chapter of this book.

CHAPTER SIX

Sloth and Neglect

A company board is the group that makes the most important strategic decisions for the company, or at least is responsible for such decisions. It is a body required to be most vigilant about corporate behaviour—a veritable Argus. But what happens when multiple eyes are closed, lulled into a false sense of security? I begin this chapter examining the nature of boards, and then move to some of the more interesting psychodynamic aspects of the way they work. Into this will be woven the story of Heath International Holdings (HIH) insurance and its disasters because the board played a major role in the HIH story; and this story was the Australian equivalent of Enron.

When HIH collapsed in early 2001, it had losses estimated at $5.3 billion. HIH was Australia's second biggest general insurer, had a big range of insurance policies covering a range of different industries and activities, but the loss was catastrophic for many people, many organisations, led to a significant bail-out by the federal government. We saw people effectively lose their livelihoods ... If I was to give just one example, HIH had extensive insurance policies covering builders, but of course when those builders couldn't get insurance because HIH had collapsed and it was very difficult to get replacement insurance, we saw enormous losses in the building industry itself. People were left with half-built homes, unable to complete these half-built homes. So in other words, although HIH itself was a

$5.3 billion loss, the losses spread throughout the Australian community.[1]

A Royal Commission, presided over by the Hon. Justice Owen produced a report in April 2003.[2] The report comments on the HIH organisational culture and the relations between management and the board. It gives a glimpse into the psychodynamics of a small group that forgot its prime purpose and failed to take up its duties. While the problems of HIH were due to poor management as well as poor governance, these are closely linked. It is the duty of a board to oversee and hold management accountable. A board is the prime partner to management. At times they may become perverse accomplices.

But, first, what is a board? A board is the group responsible for the governance of the organisation.

> Corporate governance describes the framework of rules, relation-ships, systems and processes within and by which authority is exercised and controlled in corporations ... [It] embraces not only the models or systems themselves but also the practices by which that exercise and control of authority is in fact effected.[3]

The idea that governance includes practices for the control and exercise of authority means that it involves issues of power, communication and group dynamics. A board has the basic structure of an association (see Chapter 5) normally led by a chairman.[4] Its role in governance is complex and contains many elements.

First, it is a *steward* for the primary purpose and values of the organisation. It should hold these values and represent them to others.

Second, the board is a *watchdog* for ethical process and outcomes. In this the board provides a model for those working in the organisation. The decisions and behaviour of the board provide a standard of personal and organisational ethics—what they're doing, how they're doing it, and what outcomes they seek, are all important.

Third, it is a *facilitator* of communication between management, membership, the community and other stakeholders. The board represents the organisation to outsiders. It provides a space for com-munication between the CEO, senior management, the membership and external bodies.

Finally, it provides *collaborative leadership* with the management and members of the organisation. A close partnership is important. This means a real partnership, not a lopsided dependency.

A report by *Business Week* in the US examines the changes to corporate boards that have occurred post-Enron.[5] After surveying many companies and corporate governance commentators they say, "Boards want curmudgeons who will act as watchdogs, not lapdogs", suggesting that prior to the Enron disaster US company boards were often ineffectual.[6] They point to a clean-up of problems such as directors sitting on too many boards, conflicts of interest and passive board inactivity with little quality evaluation. The lessons from disasters such as that at HIH in Australia are that boards need to be alert, independent, committed and active. However, despite the conscious efforts by those companies that recognise the problems and wish to correct or avoid them, the examination needs to go deeper to discover some of the pitfalls open to boards.

Sloth and the HIH Story

Not all the stories from HIH were about corruption, embezzlement, or anything of that ilk. HIH's problem was that subtle and unconscious processes were operating—assumptions, unspoken agreements, turning a blind eye. The board gave in to pressure and responded with fear and withdrawal from their responsibilities. The CEO retained a narcissistic and overbearing outlook. To understand what occurred does not require that we understand the big financial issues. We need to understand what happens between people in close group settings. In this case, the board neglected its duty and became lazy about its processes.

HIH was established in 1968 as a private company by Raymond Williams and Michael Payne. Williams was CEO of the company from the inception and Payne was CEO of their UK operations until 1997.[7] The company began as HIH Winterthur International Holdings but changed its name to HIH Insurance in 1998 following the withdrawal of Winterthur, the major shareholder. Even at that time there were warnings given by insurance analysts at Merrill Lynch and J P Morgan that HIH was in danger.[8] But these went unheeded. Geoffrey Cohen was the board chair from 1992 to 2001.

At a business level, the problem with HIH was that they were underreserving. Their estimate of claims on past policies were underpriced and could not be met. It wasn't that the money had been taken, or embezzled, it was that it had never been there. Throughout the story of HIH, it becomes evident that the nature and extent of the lack of adequate reserves was not understood by the board. They did not have adequate information. They did not demand the detail of information required to exercise due diligence.

The organisation was seriously mismanaged. There was a lack of attention to detail, a lack of accountability for performance and a lack of integrity in their internal processes. Management and the board lacked in their stewardship duties. For example, they did not examine the risks that they were taking. HIH re-entered the American market after a few years' absence when the board knew nothing whatever about the risks involved in this. The company was out of touch with changes there and the board asked no detailed questions. The company set up in the UK, an environment that neither management nor the board knew anything about, and they made little attempt to examine what they were committing the company to.

> The board minutes in the first half of 1993 do not disclose any consideration by the board as to whether the opening of a branch in the UK was compatible with HIH's broader strategy. There was no evidence that the board contributed to the development of a business plan for the new branch. That complacency by the board when HIH was entering unfamiliar territory, namely the UK insurance market, was inappropriate.[9]

They made huge losses. By 1996 they reported losses of A$350 million from the UK operations.[10] Beyond this, many of their assests were overestimated and lost to scrutiny inside various re-insurance agreements.

HIH acquired FAI insurance, much overpriced, widely rumoured to be shaky despite an unqualified audit report by Arthur Andersen and one of their major mistakes.[11] Also, despite advice from their own financial advisers HIH did not show due diligence in investigating FAI. Gottliebsen describes the combined risk involved in the acquisition as a potent cocktail.[12] Rodney Adler, Managing Director of FAI, who, after its acquisition by HIH became an HIH board member, was an entrepreneur, good at promoting but with a careless attitude towards risk—over-relying heavily on cash income from premiums before claims had to be paid, that is, gambling that minimal reserves would cover liabilities. He resisted all attempts to investigate FAI prior to the acquisition. This is unsurprising since it was found in the investigation into the HIH collapse that FAI was also severely underreserved and that Adler had failed to fully inform his board of the situation.

During the acquisition of FAI, the questioning, the thinking by the board, was cursory. The 1998 September board meeting called to make a decision about the acquisition was done hurriedly with little notice to the board. Five of the 12 members were absent overseas with no notice of the meeting. It was agreed to proceed without their presence. Of the remaining seven, four participated through a video link and lacked some critical documentation. In the evidence given to the Royal Commission, one board member said that he was under the impression that CEO Ray Williams had made up his mind to acquire FAI before the meeting. For him it was a *fait accompli*. Another said that he gained the impression that Williams knew Adler well and recalled that Williams had said there would be no due diligence on the acquisition. The reason was that Adler had refused this and consequently it should be considered a hostile takeover, but that the books were in order and HIH could estimate benefits of $30–$40 million per annum. This was despite another member telling the board that an analysis of the benefits of the takeover could only be cursory as there was no knowledge of FAI's costs.[13] Despite board members saying that they had previously talked about acquiring FAI, the decision was taken in circumstances of haste and with a lack of critical information.

Williams claimed during the investigation that he simply trusted the Andersen auditors. The board followed Williams with little questioning. There was:

a blind faith in a leadership that was ill-equipped for the task. There was insufficient ability and independence of mind in and associated with the organisation to see what had to be done, had to be stopped, or had to be avoided. Risks were not properly identified and managed, unpleasant information was hidden, filtered, or sanitised, and there was a lack of sceptical questioning or analysis when and where it mattered.[14]

Late in 2000 HIH became committed to a joint venture with Allianz Australia Limited, which involved selling its profitable retail businesses. This would give HIH $200 million cash to support its reserves. Neither management nor the board, however, did a thorough analysis of the cash flow implications of this alliance and it eventuated that the joint venture faced HIH with severe cash flow problems. Board members were not told of the joint venture proposal until after a memorandum had gone out to interested parties. Williams arranged an informal dinner where he discussed the matter with some of the board, but the evidence of the directors at the Royal Commission shows that some of those present recalled nothing of this discussion. Within ten weeks of the joint venture HIH was in provisional liquidation.[15] Late in 2000 Williams stepped down as CEO and was replaced by Randolph Wein, another long-term manager and HIH's Asia region chief. He was given a brief to save the company, but it was past saving and collapsed within four months of his taking the post. Moreover, the Royal Commission was informed that during the insurer's final days, Wein authorised millions of dollars in payments to HIH's directors, lawyers and consultants. He denied knowing that the collapse of the company was imminent. Wein was killed in a traffic accident in Hong Kong in October 2002.

In all this, there is a range of poor governance issues that can be identified. Primarily, the board failed to appreciate the major risks to the company through its underreserving.

This failure was evident in several forms.

a) The board neither formally received a long-term strategy for analysis, nor did they demand one. The HIH Royal Commission shows that few requests were made for a plan. It seems that knowledge of company direction and strategy was mostly gained informally. Cohen claimed that it was the management's duty to decide strategy and the board's duty to approve this in general. But, this "general view" was weak and simply involved a vision of international growth, with little detailed understanding of the risks involved.

b) The board was given little information about major strategic decisions such as acquisitions and failed to adequately explore the financial implications of such decisions. For instance, the Audit Committee "operated as no more than an extension of the board meeting and did not give separate, closer consideration to audit issues".[16] The flow of information to the board was poor, extremely so in the case of non-executive directors. The executive directors, especially Williams dominated the proceedings. The same agenda was used again and again, meetings just went through the motions and the board members did not challenge this.

c) There was lack of independence and critical analysis by the board. Two board members did raise concerns about the FAI acquisition. These were ignored or set aside by the chairman who did not want to raise issues without the imprimatur of the CEO. His anxiety to please Williams is evident. For example, Cohen did raise the issue of the small number of directors present at the 1998 September board meeting and the rushed nature of the decision about the FAI acquisition, but withdrew when Williams pushed the need to hold the meeting due to the fear that other interests in acquiring FAI might intervene.

d) Importantly, there were "no clearly defined limits to the authority of the CEO in areas such as investments, corporate donations, gifts and staff emoluments".[17] There was a failure to bring the CEO to account or even to fully examine his decisions. The organisation had started as a small private company and had since then behaved as if that was what it continued to be and the boss could say and do whatever he wanted. Williams' big spending was notorious in Australian company circles. Gottliebsen comments:

In HIH's nine years as an Australian public company, Williams seemed untrammelled by any of the normal scrutiny that is brought on a CEO by his or her board. The company was run as a series of fiefdoms with little cross communication except via Williams. Corporate governance was weak at HIH and its shareholders paid the ultimate penalty.[18]

The failure to carry out due diligence and its duties of stewardship were reflected in process. The board was conducted in a sloppy manner. There was a lack of process, and no policies or guidelines in many areas where it counted. Sometimes the guidelines that had been established were disregarded. There were conflicts of interest and no procedures for ensuring their disclosure. Either there was a complete misunderstanding of the nature of conflict of interest, or the lack of concern displayed flew in the face of such knowledge. "One director considered his personal interests were so well known that in some instances he did not have to declare an interest in a transaction to which the company was also a party."[19]

The way in which we think about authority is important. Good authority is not authoritarianism, that is, authority with no bounds.[20] Authority is that power that informs the way in which we take up the responsibility for making decisions on behalf of others. That is what boards do. And when decisions are made on behalf of others, it is encumbent upon the board to know what those others want and to understand what is in the best interests of those others. This is the duty of representation. The HIH board failed in this duty of representation to its shareholders.

In this, purpose and task are critical. What is the purpose of the organisation? How can the board run with that, sustain that, and avoid being distracted into things that divert its attention away from the main task? Sometimes boards need to take a fresh look at the purposes and the tasks of the organisation. They may have to redefine the task in light of purpose.[21] But the HIH board lacked a coherent picture of purpose. Future strategy appeared to be discussed primarily outside of board meetings or in an ad hoc way. In the event of the Allianz joint venture, board members heard only after official communication had already been publicised.

If the representational authority and responsibility of a board involves questions of purpose, task, ethics and values what does this say about the relation of boards to management? Countries differ in the details of how boards are linked to management. In the US, CEOs are selected by the board, often become the board chairman and through this role hold great power with the board.[22] According to Taylor, Chait and Holland the old system used to be that management defined the problems, the board set the policy, there were permanent structures, that meetings were process-driven, and that the board was a collection of stars.[23] The stars referred to are often hand picked by the CEO for their potential loyalty to his or her plans. These authors claim that a new approach is required where a collaborative exploration of the issues is the foundation for a relation between board and management. They suggest that there needs to be more connection between the management and the board.

In Australia, even where the roles of chair and CEO are mostly separated, independence of the board cannot be guaranteed. This is the clear lesson of the HIH case, where the board simply did what management wanted. With a more collaborative arrangement and clear independence, both management and the board should set the policy and implement it, working together. Structures should be flexible. Rather than having meetings follow the same processes every time, they should be goal-driven, so that each meeting of the group follows the needed agenda of the company's current and future directions. This is anxiety-provoking, because it feels safe and secure to imagine, as the HIH board did, that meetings will always follow the same path and the same agenda and that there won't be a need to think about anything very much because the leader will direct. One of the HIH directors noted his belief that the board agenda was inadequate for their needs in his evidence to the Royal Commission. Despite the knowledge of this, nothing was done.

At HIH the CEO's plans were followed without question. Why? Was it just because board members felt that Williams knew what he was doing, or was it also through a fear of questioning decisions made and what it was that the company was doing? And did the fear, together with the comforts gained through "mateship" lead to an organisational form of sloth—lethargy and laziness?[24]

> Williams hired the company's senior executives and hand-picked its directors; the non-executive directors—supposed to bring independent scrutiny to the company's operations—were all "mates". Williams did what he liked, treating even his majority shareholder the Swiss Winterthur group, with contempt. His big personal spending was legendary in Australian business.[25]

Greed cannot be discounted.

> Against that background [of escalating cash flow problems in the wake of the Allianz joint venture] there occurred an incident that I find quite startling. At a meeting of the board's human resources committee on 26th February 2001 it was resolved to recommend to the board retrospective increases in directors' fees. The board approved the recommendation on that day. As it turned out, there

were no adverse consequences from the decision because no payments were made under the new arrangements. But, given what the directors knew about the cash flow difficulties the company was experiencing, quite how the question of fee increases came to be considered at all—let alone approved—is a mystery to me.[26]

But greed is just one part. Scrutiny of the HIH story shows that a close collusive process was occurring in the board. Everyone was a "mate" of everyone else. The mateship and fear of its loss was a large part of the non-questioning. No one wanted to be cast out from the in-group. Hubris in the leader was supported by his mates. The directors were acting selfishly, with little concern for accountability beyond themselves. This collusion went beyond the board.

Of the seven directors of the board of HIH, three had strong links with Arthur Andersen. The Chairman, Geoffrey Cohen, was a former senior partner of the accounting firm. So was its chief financial officer, Dominic Fodera. As was another director, Justin Gardiner.[27]

The extent to which this is a picture of conscious, deliberate corruption can be questioned. Justice Owen says,

I gained the impression that the general approach of the board and of senior management was unduly deferential. No doubt it was in most cases subconscious, and it would come as a surprise to some of those involved that an outside observer would hold such a view.[28]

Eventually, Williams and Adler faced the courts and received jail sentences.

Ray Williams pleaded guilty to three criminal offences that carried maximum penalties in total of 12 years. Essentially, first of all, breaches of his duty as a Director of HIH; But also the other two offences to which he pleaded guilty, went to breaches of disclosure laws, in particular, he, if you like, knew that information in a prospectus was misleading, was incorrect, and also an Annual Report of HIH seriously overestimated the operating profit of HIH to the extent of something like $92 million. He pleaded guilty to knowing that that information, when it went to the public, was incorrect.

Rodney Adler pleaded guilty to four criminal offences. Each of those carried a maximum term of imprisonment of five years, in other words, a maximum term of imprisonment of 20 years. Those offences went to breaches of directors' duties also, but they also went to Rodney Adler if you like, participating in once again, provision of false information, in one instance, giving false information to a journalist at the *Financial Review*, effectively that Rodney Adler himself was investing in shares in HIH. It turned out that that was not the case at all, Rodney Adler was not using his own money to invest in these shares, he was in fact using funds that he'd obtained from HIH, which in itself was not legal.[29]

Cohen has since been charged with misleading shareholders in a meeting in December 2000, but judgment has not yet come down on his case. In legal terms, the crimes of these men were not about the collapse of the company as the corporation takes responsibility for mismanagement, not individuals.[30] Their crimes were the lies and misleading information that they put out when they knew about the severe problems that the company was having. Their crimes were in their lies and cover-up. Public fury was strong. People spat at Adler in the street.

The psychodynamics of the case show more than just a criminal cover-up by a few people, but also a case of groupthink.[31] The organisational culture in the board led to failure in the first instance due to the absence of adequate risk assessment and due diligence. The perverse pride and arrogance of Williams and Adler was present in their failure to see the problems confronting them. Williams' domination of the board members and careful grooming of them to his own taste, led to a perverse sloth in the board. It was a case of corporate lemmings. The leaders knew of the problems but failed to acknowledge the extent of their risks. The board was created and kept as a perverse accomplice.

Neglect: Ansett Airlines

Ansett suffered from the effects of corporate neglect, gross mismanagement and interfering governments on both sides of the Tasman.[32]

Ansett Airlines began as an Australian privately owned company, Ansett Airways Pty. Ltd in 1935, founded by Sir Reginald Ansett. But in 2001 the company had a major crisis and went into collapse. Ansett was a major player in the Australian domestic flight market for nearly seven decades. For many years two airlines dominated the scene: between 1946 and 1986 the two were Ansett and Trans-Australian Airlines (TAA) a government-owned company. TAA later became Australian Airlines between 1986 and 1992. It was bought by Qantas in 1993, which itself was privatised in 1995. Ansett remained a private competitor throughout this time. It was highly successful. Over this period, the two airlines roughly took 50 per cent each of the domestic market. The highly regulated environment provided by the Australian Government saved Australian airlines from the sort of bankruptcies suffered by airlines around the world, especially in the US, where, because of the unregulated market there, investment guru Warren Buffett gives the advice not to invest in airlines. But this was not the case in Australia. The two airline systems did well. The staff of Ansett were seen as dedicated and the company made many innovations in service. Ansett was reaching into the international market, flying to Asia and the Pacific. What, then, went wrong?

At the time of Ansett's closure its fleet was antiquated, in need of upgrading and required high degrees of maintenance. The airline had changed ownership several times and each of the owners had failed to listen to its management's requests for an injection of funds to make the necessary upgrades.[33] It seems each buyer just wanted to take what they could from this once prosperous company, putting little back in. News Corporation bought into Ansett in the 1980s. Later TNT's Sir Peter Abeles became an owner and the airline was jointly run by News Corporation and TNT.

While Sir Reg Ansett laid the groundwork for a national icon, Sir Peter Abeles took it by the scruff of the neck and laid the groundwork for disaster. A hard, tough businessman he may have been . . . a visionary airline chief he was not. Abeles was a one-man autocracy: he ran on hunch, hardly listened to advisers and went off to air shows in Paris and London, returning with bags full of aircraft ordered with little reference to company planners.[34]

Air New Zealand bought TNT's 50 per cent in 1996. Then, in March 2000, Air New Zealand became sole owners after buying News Corporation's 50 per cent share. Gottliebsen describes the purchase as having doomed the airline.

I chatted to the then Ansett CEO, Rod Eddington, who sounded optimistic about the potential, but his eyes told the story. It had been driven by Cushing, who, while one of the best judges of wine in New Zealand, seemed to have little concept of what would be required for Air NZ to own the much bigger Ansett. His CEO McCrea looked and sounded out of his depth.[35]

Mc Crea stepped down as CEO just before Air New Zealand took control, leaving the whole show leaderless for over four months. Moreover, Air New Zealand had paid too much for the airline, and its executives were faced with a task beyond their capacities.

Then Ansett's woes worsened, with a series of maintenance and safety lapses in its ageing fleet that grounded its 767s and left passengers stranded at Christmas and Easter. By June this year (2001), Air New Zealand itself was desperate for capital to replenish the fleet and save Ansett. Singapore Airlines offered to increase its 25% shareholding in Air New Zealand—and inject the needed capital—but the major hurdle was the New Zealand Government—intransigent on any increase in foreign ownership of its national carrier. The New Zealand Government delayed, then rejected Singapore's proposal. Ansett's fate was probably sealed at that time. This week, Air New Zealand announced the biggest corporate loss in New Zealand history.[36]

Finally the airline was grounded and several attempts to save it failed. Sixteen thousand Ansett employees lost out; as did many employees in associated industries. Five years on, the receiver was still paying out small sums. They are worth little now, badly gnawed by inflation.

Too often in the history of Ansett we hear of owners who fail to listen to those who knew the business best—the management and staff. There is a picture of arrogance, anger and whim; of the airline simply being the possession, pawn even, of distant players—a personal item. Gottliebsen describes, for example, how Singapore Airlines chief was "livid" when his offer to buy the Newscorp shares lost to Air New Zealand whose offer was by no means as promising. The rejection was felt to be an insult and, according to my reading, seems to have been taken personally. The sale to Air New Zealand was not a good one for the airline. And, a later rejection by the New Zealand Government angered Singapore Inc., the consortium of Singaporese financial backers; the multinationals feeling that they should not be constrained by governments. But even within Australia, TNT's Peter Abeles took on the airline as a toy, his life's desire.[37] Linsey Fox, trucking magnate, and millionaire businessman Solomon Lew, two of Ansett's would be rescuers, pulled out from their rescue deal at the last minute in January 2002. One gets the picture of the airline as an orphan buffeted by ill fortune due to a line of uncaring foster parents. But more so, because of the protection of Australian Government regulation, it was an orphan neglected in times of plenty. So, why?

The Dynamics

Dominating the stories of HIH Insurance and Ansett Airlines are the larger than life characters of multinational entrepreneurs; generally wealthy men who are used to getting their own way, often convinced, perhaps through a series of successes, that they are right and are little in need of the advice of others—until arrogant risks overshoot the mark, or gambles fail to pay out. Hidden in the stories are their counterparts. These are the directors and senior managers who become accomplices in their leaders' pride and greed through their own failure to question and hold to their watchdog role. In addition, as Sykes points out, the professional bodies such as the audit and accounting firms also become accomplices.[38] The professional bodies who should hold the members of these firms to account fail to do so. Too often fear and their own accompanying ambition prompts boards and professional bodies to stay silent when they should not; or sloth engulfs them when the going looks easy. Such dynamics seem more in place in the court of England's sixteenth-century Henry VIII than in the modern boardrooms of twenty-first-century multinational corporations. But group dynamics and organisational cultures are as subject now to the effects of primitive emotions as they have ever been.

There is little written about laziness or sloth in the literature about organisational psychodynamics, although it could be argued that depression, much discussed, may lie behind lethargy. But I am not convinced that the issues discussed in this chapter are linked to depression. Depression is more likely the result of repressed anger. I believe the dynamic we are describing here is one of disengagement from the organisation and turning into apathy.

In broad social terms, apathy is popularly seen as a form of moral lassitude and linked to the general breakdown of the authority held by traditional institutions such as the Church, paternalism and bureaucracy. Generally religions see laziness as a sin. One idea being that justice must be done to God's creation, using skills and capabilities to the full, while laziness fails in this. Sloth can be popularly defined as:

> laziness; idleness and wastefulness of time allotted. Laziness is condemned because:
>
> - others have to work harder
> - it is disadvantageous for oneself, because useful work does not get done
> - an equilibrium: one does not produce much, but one does not need much either (in Dante's theology, sloth is the "failure to love God with all one's heart, all one's mind, and all one's soul"—specific examples including laziness, cowardice, lack of imagination, complacency, and irresponsibility).[39]

The recent rise of religious fundamentalism can be viewed partly as a movement against apathy and its evil effects, attempting to bring back meaning in a world where sloth grows heavily on top of greed. But, even from a humanist and non-religious perspective, laziness may be viewed negatively as an escape from confronting the difficulties of self-knowledge. It is seen in complacency and irresponsibility. In this sense it is a psychic retreat from inner knowledge and reality.

In terms of the perverse dynamics examined in this book, laziness is seen to be the disease of the accomplice. It is the psychodynamic involved in the turning of a blind eye by board members, senior managers, professional bodies or other stakeholders who don't want to stand out from the crowd, who don't want to disturb the status quo through posing hard questions, who don't want to get powerful leaders off-side, or who simply don't want to put in the effort required. And, at times, it is an easy role to slip into, neither consciously nor deliberately, but blindly, because it is the role of the mass follower, without thought. This can occur even in a small group such as a company board.

Rather than seeing the dynamic as simply due to lazy individuals, the culture needs to be considered first and foremost. The accomplice is the collectivity. HIH board members, it seems, were selectively lazy, choosing not to attend to the risks that they should have been bound to attend to. Individual dissenting voices were not heard. The collectivity chose to follow Williams out of general loyalty, fear and self-interest. Such behaviour was habitual. The culture allowed, even encouraged, individual laziness to emerge and dominate certain actions and decisions. Group laziness is that state of perverse "not-knowing"; a collusive refusal to know or to pursue and examine the truth.

At this stage it is worth further examining the psychodynamics of denial. Chapter 2 looked at the Freudian idea of the origins of denial as a defence against the anxiety of castration. In essence, this explanation sees denial as a turning away from a thought; the thought of a potentially severe narcissistic blow. Denial, then, is a psychic mechanism that dismisses thoughts. But, thoughts have an insistence because they come from the symbolic world of language and culture, an outside reality, even though they seem to emerge inside one's head.[40] Lacan, Bion and Lawrence each describe the emergence of thoughts from outside the individual thinker. They understand their emergence in the social sphere of the Symbolic field,[41] or the infinite.[42] We may entertain and use thoughts through the process of thinking and in this process we may distort them and give them a consciousness out of touch with their social reality—we may even create lies. In this way, thinking is an impure filter, at times good enough, at other times, contaminating.

The capacity to think, that is, to use this filter, appears to come from a relation to reality that is frustrating. If all wishes were satisfied immediately, there would be no need to think. But, because there are delays between what is desired and its satisfaction, there arises the psychic mechanism of imagery and representation. The wished for satisfaction is imagined and gives temporary relief. Moreover, there is something in the nature of desire that can never be satisfied. So relief is temporary and desire gives rise to an increasing need for representation of satisfactions. There are many theories in psychoanalysis that examine how thinking arises[43] but, essentially, there is concurrence about the idea that representational thinking arises from an absence; from a gap between desire and satisfaction. For the infant the representation is of a past satisfaction.[44] But, once the child has entered the social world, conscious representations are forever marked by language and the particular logic of the culture surrounding the thinker.[45] Thinking is inevitably a group process, even though it is carried out by individuals.

So, I return to my argument about the *insistence* of thoughts. This brings back the notion that denial turns away from thought. The more the thought insists, the more vehement must be the denial. Bion asks that the psychoanalyst place himself in a state of "not-knowing" following the ideas of Keats on negative capability.[46] This allows the psychoanalyst to approach his patients free of misleading memories, desires and understandings. But, the "not-knowing" of denial is not the disinterested stance of the scientist or psychoanalyst who embraces "not-knowing" for purposes of objectivity or freedom from prejudice. It is a "not-knowing" that actively blocks and attacks thought. This is not a simple turning away, but an active rejection. So, if group laziness is a perverse "not-knowing" the dynamic is not naive. It is not the lethargy of simple tiredness. Instead of examining the thoughts that come to it, the lazy board pushes them out and away. This turning away is an actively destructive force.

What of the accompanying issue of neglect? Neglect may be due to laziness but at times neglect can be more wilful, a result of deliberate abandonment. Yet, again, neglect may be the result of a blindness about the real needs of the neglected party. Were the various owners of Ansett neglectful due to self-interest and greed, wanting to screw every last dollar from what was once an Australian icon? Were there any attempts to deliberately run down the company? Or, was neglect also due to a captivating fantasy that this airline could survive without being nourished; that it was somehow immortal? To take up the image of the neglected child, lost while the quarrelling parents go about the business of serving their own interests, it could be said that Ansett was regarded as a golden child able to survive in and of itself without due parental vigilance and nurture.

In a strange parallel to the Ansett company story, the story of the Ansett family also involves neglect and betrayal. Sir Reginal Ansett, founder of the company neglected to keep in contact with the sons from his first marriage. The first wife and sons moved to the US while he remarried and had three daughters with his new wife. The sons were not contacted and only twice received a letter from their father in 17 years. Lady Ansett, the new wife was reputed to want nothing to do with this first family and actively kept the two families apart— to the extent that she attempted to keep the sons from attending their father's funeral, years later. When Bob Ansett, the older son, returned to Australia and successfully and independently founded Budget car rentals, he met his father for a few clandestine lunches "not as father and son, but as adults".[47] Still wanting his father's approval, although never getting any help, the son outlined to his father his business strategy for winning exclusive car rental rights at Melbourne airport. This was the last time they met. The next week found Sir Reginald as new owner of Avis car rentals, Budget's chief rival in the airport deal. The betrayal was astounding and put in the name of "business comes first".

But beyond this, the elder daughter from the second marriage lived with her husband for many years in a cottage on the large family estate where she stood as background support for Lady Ansett in her declining years. After her mother's death, she learned that her father's will left nothing to his children. Ansett Airlines or any other company interest was out of the picture now, but the personal estate was still large. The family estate was sold. Even the cottage was not left to the daughter. Sir Reginald believed that his children had to make it alone, like he did. This might be understood as a rationalisation.

This family story, like that of Gucci reported by Stein[48] is, perhaps, also a case of anger and envy (see Chapter 5) as well as neglect.

Notes

1. Ian Ramsay: HIH—The First Legal Scalps; ABC Law Report; 19 April 2005.
2. Justice Owen, N. (2003). Report of the Royal Commission into the Collapse of HIH. *The Failure of HIH Insurance Volumes 1&2: A corporate collapse and its lessons.* Canberra: Commonwealth of Australia Canberra Publishing and Printing.
3. Justice Owen (2003), op. cit., Vol. 1, p. x.
4. Generic term to cover both genders.
5. The case of Enron is examined briefly in Chapter 2 of this book.
6. *Business Week* Special Report, *The Best and Worst Boards*, 7 October 2002, p. 108.
7. Other senior managers and board members were George Suresteps and Terence Cassidy who had joined the company in the first years of its operation, and Dominic Fodera and Randolph Wayne. Non-executive directors named in the Royal Commission report were Geoffrey Cohen (the chair), Charles Abbott, Rodney Adler (who joined the board after the acquisition of FAI, another insurance company) Justin Gardiner, Alexander Gorrie, Neville Head and Robert Stitt.
8. Gottliebsen, R. (2003). *10 Best and 10 Worst Decisions of Australian CEOs 1992–2002*. Camberwell, Australia: Viking, Penguin Group.
9. Justice Owen (2003), op. cit., Vol. 2 [23.3.1].
10. Gottliebsen, R. (2003), op. cit.
11. Sykes, T. (2006). "Address to a Quadrant dinner", published in *Quadrant*, May 2006.
12. Gottliebsen, R. (2003), op. cit.
13. Justice Owen (2003), op. cit., Vol. 2. Details of the investigation and the evidence of the directors is given here.
14. Justice Owen (2003), op. cit., Vol. 1, p. iii.
15. Justice Owen (2003), op. cit., Vol. 1.
16. Justice Owen (2003), op. cit., Vol. 2 [23.2].
17. Ibid., p. xviii.
18. Gottliebsen, R. (2003), op. cit., p. 190.
19. Justice Owen (2003), op. cit., Vol. 1, p. xx.
20. See Hoggett, P., Mayo, M. and Miller, C. (2006). "On Good Authority". *Socio-Analysis*, 8: 1–16 for a discussion of the nature of authority.
21. An example of redefining task in light of purpose occurred when I was working with a local government authority. The people who

were organising childcare wanted to think about "What is it that we really do? What do we want to offer the community?" They thought of "Looking after small children" and "Helping to educate as well as care", and so on, and were struggling with this until an engineer at the back of the room said "Well, what you're really doing is giving parents peace of mind". This enabled the group to rethink their task because of input from someone coming from an entirely different area. "If we think about giving the parents peace of mind as well as supporting the children, that means we'd think differently about what we're doing and how we're doing it."

22. Eisold, K. (2003). "Corrupt Groups in Contemporary Corporations: Outside boards and inside traders". Paper given at the ISPSO Symposium "Power and Politics in Organisations" Boston, June. Eisold argues "We get the CEOs we deserve . . . we allow ourselves to become blinded" (p. 16) referring both to the past when CEOs were idealised and also now when they are being blamed for corporate failures. He emphasises the role the system has in collaborating with the CEO. The idealisation of the CEO was part of the HIH picture.
23. Taylor, B.E., Chait, R.P. and Holland, T.P. (1996). "The New Work of the Non Profit Board". *HBR September–October 1996*.
24. In Australian culture, mateship refers to the close friendship bonds between (usually) men. Loyalty to mates is highly valued and expected.
25. Gottliebsen, R. (2003), op. cit., p. 190.
26. Justice Owen (2003), op. cit., p. xxiii.
27. Roi, E. *Impact on HIH Auditors*. ABC PM program 17 May 2001.
28. Justice Owen (2003), op. cit., Vol. 1, p. xiii.
29. Ian Ramsay: HIH—The First Legal Scalps; ABC Law Report; 19 April 2005.
30. Ralston Saul, J. (1997). *The Unconscious Civilization*. Harmondsworth: Penguin Books.
31. Janis, I.L. (1986). *Victims of Groupthink: A psychological study of foreign policy decisions and fiascos*. Boston, MA: Houghton Mifflin.
32. http://sunday.ninemsn.com.au/sunday/feature_stories/article_924.
33. Ballantyne, T. (2002). "What Really went Wrong at Ansett?" www.spiritsofansett.com/history/ballantyne.htm.
34. Ibid.
35. Gottliebsen, R. (2003), op. cit., p. 162.

36. http://sunday.ninemsn.com.au/sunday/feature_stories/article_924, 2001.
37. Ballantyne, T. (2002), op. cit.
38. Sykes, T. (2006), op. cit.
39. http://en.wikipedia.org/wiki/User:WBardwin/claypit. This internet dictionary reports popular rather than scholarly definitions.
40. The notion of thoughts belonging not to individuals but to the group seems counter-intuitive to many people. But if you consider language as belonging to the group rather than to the individual, more sense can be gained. Language belongs to the collective. It is collectively created and changed over time. Individuals use the language available in their culture, with its rules and meanings. Individually created language doesn't work. The group must take up innovations or the individual is left isolated with his or her own idiosyncratic sounds. Thoughts can be regarded also in this way.
41. Lacan, J. (1977). *Ecrits*. London: Tavistock Publications.
42. Lawrence, W.G. (1998). "Won from the void and formless infinite". In: W.G. Lawrence (ed.) *Social Dreaming @ Work*. London: Karnac Books.
43. Long, S. (2000b). "Engaging the Task: A socio-analytic discussion of task presence and absence". *Socio-Analysis*, 2 (1): 80–101.
44. Freud, S. (1900). *The Interpretation of Dreams*. Edited by James Strachey and revised by Angela Richards, The Pelican Freud Library, Harmondsworth: Penguin Books, 1976.
45. Sullivan, H.S. (1950). "The Illusion of Personal Individuality". *Psychiatry*, 13: 317–32. Lacan, J. (1977), op. cit.
46. Bion, W. (1970). *Attention and Interpretation*. London: Tavistock Publications.
47. Bob Ansett's words—"Dynasties" programme on the Australian Broadcasting Corporation (ABC), 28 November 2006.
48. Stein, M. (2005). "The Othello Conundrum: The inner contagion of leadership". *Organization Studies*, 26 (9): 1405–19.

CHAPTER SEVEN

Perverse Wrath

On the second of February 2003 a reportedly friendly, supportive and good natured 20-year-old army trainee at the Singleton Trainee School of Infantry, Australia, hanged himself shortly after midnight. Two weeks previously, only one week into his infantry training course he had injured his leg in a training exercise. Following the accident, after several tests, "he was diagnosed with a stress-related condition, but was cleared of stress fractures. On 28 Jan 03 he was removed from training and transferred to Rehabilitation and Discharge Platoon (R&DPl) in order to recuperate."[1]

This period of recuperation proved to be the beginning of the road towards his suicide. During the investigation it was found that on the evening before his death he had altercations with two other trainees. In addition, he had become depressed and had drunk heavily. He was found hanging from a tree behind the R&D lines early the next morning. What would drive this young man to such an action?

The investigation reports several allegations brought against the army by Private Williams' family. Among these were allegations about a culture of denigration at the army recruit training centre, a culture of bullying and denigration at the School of Infantry and a widespread usage of abusive and offensive language. These allegations were upheld. It was also found that the rehabilitation facility where he had been sent after his injury was inadequately staffed and that there was inadequate medical treatment and rehabilitation support. The rehabilitation centre was located close to the training facility and those "recuperating" were thus in close contact with the prevailing training culture, training officers and trainees. Little real respite from the culture was available. There were also allegations of threats of physical violence, intimidation and standover tactics by both staff and trainees against other trainees. Some staff were said to be specifically targetting individual trainees, marking them for failure. Although this allegation was not found by the investigating officer to be commonplace in the culture, individual instances were found. How many reported instances it would take for a judgement of "commonplace" to occur was not discussed.

Much of the harassment and denigration was aimed at those considered "weak". Having an injury that potentially might lead to a case for discharge came into this category. Those showing vulnerability were targeted with denigrating innuendo, the implication being that their illnesses or injuries were self-inflicted with the intent of getting taken off the course. It appeared to be general thinking that those with injuries might be course "failures" wanting to get out. The fact that those in rehabilitation were transferred to the rehabilitation and discharge platoon indicates the link between injury and discharge.

Private Williams, it seems, held concerns that he might be viewed in this light—not because this was his intent, or because he was failing, but, because this was an expectation that anyone with an injury might have entertained given the prevailing culture. Although it was claimed that Private Williams was reassured that his injuries were not serious and he had no cause to believe that he would be discharged, it must be remembered that professional support was thin on the ground and psychological counselling not readily available. Reading between the lines of the report, a picture emerges of a young man caught in an unremittingly aggressive culture, with many others ready to find scapegoats who could be deemed "weak" in order that they could, by contrast, see themselves as "strong" and thus evade any denigration falling their way. The rehabilitation centre itself became a place not of relief and support, but a new hell.

In light of the findings about the culture, the leadership came under scrutiny. It was judged that the Commanding Officer was "over tasked and under resourced". His attention was not sufficiently on the training. In fact, it was apparent that the senior officers at times turned a blind eye. There were claims that those further up the chain of command were unaware of the culture of the School of Infantry, that it was a legacy from the past, believed no longer to be in place. However, only two years previously there had been an investigation into the school. The officer investigating the death of Private Williams comments on this prior report:

> An investigation was completed in 2001 following a submission to the Minister regarding the alleged mistreatment of PTE XX at SOI in 2000. The investigation identified a culture at SOI with distinct similarities to that described in this report. It also noted that as a result of changes in 2000/01, there was a far more professional and positive attitude at SOI. These changes and the apparent resolution of the problem also bear a remarkable similarity to the findings of this report.[2]

It seems that the earlier investigation bore little fruit in the way of changing the culture. Questions had been raised and promises made, but two years on, the same issues were present. A belief by senior staff that the issue had been solved was now either denial or wishful thinking—at least, perhaps, a wish that the situation no longer be an irritant for the school through public focus. Private Williams' death instigated a new set of questions and promises. For instance, following the investigation anonymous questionnaires were to be given to all trainees leaving the School of Infantry to record all instances of breaches of the army code of conduct.[3] Such a move was put in place as an attempt to root out those individuals who constantly broke the code which "forbids the humiliation or belittling of trainees or subordinates, or their subjection to physical, verbal and sexual abuse;"[4] a code sorely needed, but whose existence itself speaks to the idea that such practices were generally occurring.

The 2003 report lists many changes to be put in place by the army following the suicide of Private Williams. But if the abusive, aggressive culture is continuously supported through the perverse culture of turning a blind eye, it is hard to see such changes as sustainable.

The Culture of Abuse

The School of Infantry at Singleton is not alone among army training establishments in its culture of bullying, denigration and intimidation. Such cultures, if not typical, are widespread. Simply key "army trainee abuse" into "Google", the internet web search engine, and you will find many, many pages of reports on abuse in a range of countries, plus articles on abuse prevention in military establishments. Here are some examples.

> Staff Sergeant Simpson sexually assaulted female trainees at Aberdeen Proving Ground (APG), Maryland, between November 1994 and September 1996. A general court-martial composed of officers and enlisted members convicted SSG Simpson and sentenced him to a dishonourable discharge, twenty-five years confinement, total forfeitures, and reduction to the grade of E-1.[5]

Staff Sergeant Simpson was only one of several accused at Aberdeen in the US, the centre of a notorious scandal involving trainee abuse. And, we find another scandalous case, this time in Britain:

> A four-year investigation by the Surrey police force into the deaths at Deepcut uncovered 173 allegations of ritual humiliation, bullying and sexual abuse including rape. These are just the abuses that were reported, and are likely to be just the tip of the iceberg. In the seven-year period covering the four deaths at Deepcut, some 12,000 recruits passed through the training regime there.[6]

And, outside the western world:

> There's a furore in Colombia at the moment over the case of 21 young soldiers cruelly tortured and beaten by their superiors in an army training camp. The head of the armed forces was forced to resign as a result, although some analysts think this is a move to ensure that those actually involved directly in the torture don't face any charges.[7]

If only a percentage of the reports listed are valid, it provides strong evidence of regular army recruit abuse, by officers and other trainees, despite the wishes of some within the army to remove this culture.[8] In light of this, it becomes not at all surprising that torture and abuse occur in situations of war—Abu Grahib prison in Iraq, for example, where prisoners of war were recently humiliated and beaten. Indeed, we might say that wars provide an opportunity for the practice of an already existent culture of abuse. Army recruits are given training in abuse first-hand through the culture of the training facilities. Abuse begets abuse.

A Necessary Culture?

Aggression is needed in order to fight. The lessons of war show that most soldiers in face-to-face armed combat need to be driven into that position either by a heightening of adrenalin and aggression or by the threat of being labelled a coward or being shot by their own officers.[9]

Training is required to overcome the natural response of flight and withdrawal. Single-minded focus is also critical for the soldier. In field training, aggression is tuned and focused through hours of drill, manoeuvres and war games. In line with such focus, hatred for "the enemy" is incited. The enemy is the alien "other", imbued with every disgusting tendency; regarded as inhumane and vicious. It seems, the darker the visage of the enemy, the purer the motives of the soldier who fights him. All this is part of the psychological "splitting" process between good and bad described by Melanie Klein.[10] It focuses the fighting intent, driving out any doubt or questioning. It is a vision of black and white. In combat to waver, to have doubt, may mean death.

But, is the training in aggressive and defensive combat a sufficient explanation for a culture of denigration and abuse?

In the training facilities, the conscious rationalisation is that abuse is not institutionally intended. Although there may be individual sadistic officers or fellow trainees, this is not the norm. In the cultural vernacular, training is required to toughen up the raw recruit for his own good and for the good of his fellows and, sometimes, that process goes too far. For example, navy recruits have been known to drown in training pools where the "sink or swim" philosophy prevailed. But the culture of abuse goes beyond this.

Other dynamics are in place. First, the fact that vulnerability is targeted supports a hypothesis of the widespread fear of vulnerability. The perceived "weak" become convenient "containers" for feelings of vulnerability that the so-called "strong" may feel but do not openly acknowledge. These include unconscious feelings of vulnerability, but sometimes such feelings may be as much consciously deflected as unconsciously projected. Fear of vulnerability is understandable, but in the culture, if not in the individual, it is—must be—denied. Rejection of vulnerability becomes an imperative. The myth of the hero, brave in the face of all adversity must be upheld. Everyone knows that all are potentially vulnerable, but they must also *not know* this, because any vulnerability unconsciously means death. The perversity of the situation begins to emerge.

Second, the need for an enemy is present. It is the sine qua non of an army. It is not simply that there *is* an enemy. There *must be* an enemy. This may be the defining factor of a paranoid culture, what Bion describes as fight/flight.[11] But even then, an enemy may be conceived of in different ways. Where fear is denied and masked, it hides behind loathing, hatred and rage. The enemy is vilified, dehumanised and, as a result of this, in many instances is underestimated. Rage against the enemy is as likely to cause self-impotence as damage to the other because it blinds one to reason when reason is most required. Where fear is acknowledged, there is a greater chance that the enemy is understood as a realistic "other" and threat is evaluated accordingly. The enemy may become a more worthy opponent—approached with careful determination rather than with rage or contempt.

In a socio-analytic analysis of vengeance, Sievers and Mersky[12] give another clue as to the nature of the masked fear. It may be largely fear of the defending group's own destructiveness and its accompanying guilt. This cannot be borne by the group and is displaced. They take up the work of Fornari.[13]

> Because groups, in a perverse and alienated way, have difficulty experiencing loss, assuming responsibility for their own destructiveness and coping with the associated guilt, they see the destructivity and annihilation they experience as caused by the environment, i.e. by an evil other group. This displacement of guilt can—according to Fornari—be interpreted as an alienated elaboration of mourning. Contrary to the non-psychotic elaboration of mourning, in which the pain of mourning can be endured by the confidence that eventually it can be overcome (Fornari, 1966/1975, p 224), the psychotic elaboration of mourning is based on feelings which are projected—as blame—onto the

enemy (ibid., 51). The destruction is seen to have been caused by an enemy who, through a process of projection, becomes the object of hatred and represents the unacknowledged guilt of those who experience attack or a fear of being attacked.[14]

If there is not an immediate enemy, what then? The modern day peacekeeping task of armies may seem to stand in contradistinction to the need for an enemy. But, even in peacekeeping there is a need for vigilance and the mobilisation of assertive aggression. The enemy is still there, but contained. Moreover, it seems in the parlance of modern western governments, for example, in the US, that we must see the enemy everywhere: in the war against drugs, the war against crime, the war against terrorism and, perhaps, the war against war. The military training grounds thus are places where psycho-dynamically, enemies must be created and then found. To be an army means to have an enemy, just as to be a teacher one must have a student. They are more than semantic role pairs, each defining the other. This is in action. The protagonist is enemy to the "other" enemy. So, in the language and practice of this culture, everyone is created as an enemy. The nature of enemies is that each fears and hates the other; each is afraid and full of rage.

Third, the presence of an enemy leads to a further dynamic. If the designated "enemy" accepts the role, the pair (protagonist and enemy) is caught together in a rage, whether cold- or hot-blooded that masks their fear. Rage and anger become the visible signs of denied feelings of vulnerability and guilt and, in this process, enemy pairs react to each other with increased intensity. René Girard illuminates this in his analysis of the dynamic of vengeance.[15] The feud, for example, demonstrates this. Here, enemy mirrors enemy as each seeks revenge for past grievances that create yet new reasons for further revenge. Examples abound in contemporary wars in the Middle East, Europe and Africa. The increasing escalation of this process, Girard argues, is only stopped by the finding of a scapegoat. The scapegoat is someone, or some group who the warring enemies, collectively and unconsciously, agree shall hold the blame for the grievances and be punished. The unwitting, most often unwilling role in the vengeance cycle is the scapegoat onto whom blame is displaced. Just as the presence of denial of fear and vulnerability hints at perversity, so the presence of an enemy, escalating rage and eventual displacement onto a scapegoat (the unconscious representative of the larger community) points towards an unwitting victim, providing more evidence of the perverse process.[16] Private Williams was, in many senses, a scapegoat in a culture of fear and sadism.

A fourth system dynamic indicates an even larger displacement. Many psychoanalysts since Freud[17] have examined the nature of the army as a social group that "holds" and represents the aggressive tendencies of the general culture. Perhaps it doesn't take a psychoanalyst to understand the role of the army as the aggressive defender of a state, or defender of any group able to muster and sustain it as a fighting body. However, the analysts have added that the army not only *fights* on behalf of others, but also experiences, expresses and exhibits aggression *for* those others.[18] It is as if the general population can absolve itself of these feelings through their projection into the armed forces and the wars in which they engage. The army culture becomes another kind of scapegoat, unconsciously holding the fears and guilt and consciously holding the aggression of the larger social body.

These four dynamics are all present in armed forces training facilities, namely: (i) the presence of fear and unconscious guilt, (ii) its masking and deflection by rage (wrath) against a created enemy, (iii) the emergence of scapegoats so the rage can be eventually displaced and dispersed and (iv) the playing out of this whole process within a specialised social group, that is, the armed forces, on behalf of us all. The question might be asked, is this whole process an example of the organisational perverse state of mind?

This can be tested against the five points put forward throughout this book. First, within a sadistic denigrating culture, certainly there is the institutionalised gaining of individual pleasure at the expense of the general good. In some situations and facilities, the culture is so entrenched that the abusive power given to the officers, and taken up by some trainees is the major source of fear experienced by trainees. The fear feeds the abuse and is savoured by the abuser. This is the nature of sadism. In the analysis put forward the fear experienced by the victim trainees is displaced from the unacknowledged fear within the system as a whole.

Second, the whole organisation is caught in the defence of denial. Senior officers turn a blind eye. Investigations uncover abuse, but little changes, as evidenced in the case presented at the beginning of this chapter. Third, accomplices are present, whether in the knowing form of fellow abusers, the officials outside the training facility who know and yet don't know, or in the form described by Girard of the unwitting and unwilling scapegoat. Fourth, there is a general culture of instrumentality. Recruits are there to serve an end on behalf of society. Finally, the abusive culture renews itself.

This whole analysis is about the perverse dynamics within armed forces training. It does not deny the fact that sometimes there are real enemies that must be faced, or that the armed forces contain good people who serve their countries with courage and valour. The argument put forward is that there are perverse dynamics within society that get played out in the armed forces' cultures. This is a dynamic for which we must all take some responsibility through our governments. There is a vital need not to get caught in the perverse process that creates enemies and fear and perverts them into an opportunity for the outpouring of rage and wrath.

Perverse Wrath and the Culture of Bullying

The issue of bullying in the workplace has become a focus for many researchers, managers and organisational consultants over the last two decades.[19] What in the past might have been regarded as "throwing one's weight around" may now be regarded seriously as abusive. Bullying ranks highly as a workplace problem, as do its more specific forms found in sexual and racial harassment. All are regarded as situations where people in power abuse their position. This is the case also when the power is derived from peer group informal power. Each is seen as a serious injustice that creates roles of perpetrator, victim and audience.[20] It's not that there were not bullies and victims in the past, there were. However, now the behaviours, the roles and the social processes surrounding them have become legitimate foci for the organisation to think about and manage—a legitimate organisational discourse, if you like. Bullying has gained a place in the theatre of organisational life and beyond because, although organisations now have several steps in the formal process of establishing the facts surrounding allegations of bullying, discovering and punishing the culprits and managing the fallout from the whole process, formal litigation through the courts is increasingly employed.

Whereas many explanations of bullying focus on the personality of the bully, perhaps arguing the role of individual history in the development of bullies seen to displace their intolerable fears and guilt onto a hapless victim, in this book, the focus is on the organisation. Interest here is on the socio-emotional conditions that give rise to perverse organisational dynamics. Can some of these be identified in the case of bullying?

First, is the condition of turning a blind eye by the authorities— senior managers, board members and regulators. They may know of the existence of a bullying culture, but choose to ignore it, just as in the examples given from military training. Getting a task completed, financial targets achieved and Key Performance Indicators (KPIs) met are all important. But, when the achievement of these targets disregards the means by which they are achieved, the door is open for abuse. An authority that ignores the means to achieving its ends is not in itself abusive, but under such conditions, perverse practices may find a place.

Such disregard in the workplace (if and when it occurs) parallels the attitude of other authorities, and concern in the workplace reflects concern in the broader society. Recent interest in bullying at work seems to fit within a broad social justice agenda, keen to discover and expose the injustices of the past and make amends. Examples are the truth and reconciliation process in South Africa, the exposure of the abuse of children in its care by segments of the Catholic Church, and the whole issue of the stolen generation of Indigenous children in Australia. All these are stories of social injustice writ large. This social trend has a mixed ambition, where some sections of the society wish to discover and expose injustices of the past, while others wish to deny that injustices were done, hoping to perpetuate past myths. Strong contenders in this latter dynamic, for example, are those who deny the historical validity of the Holocaust, enacting perverse dynamics on a huge socio-historic stage.

An emphasis on reconciliation seems the positive side to the concern about abusive social situations. It is an alternative to the cycle of vengeance with its need for scapegoats. A process named "restorative justice" implemented in many modern justice systems attempts this. It is used especially within juvenile justice, where offenders are faced with the consequences of their crimes in relation to their victims and reconciliation, of sorts, becomes part of the offender's treatment programme and the victim's recovery. Restorative justice has two basic forms.[21] The first is the process of bringing together "all those affected by the crime to discuss what has happened and to agree on what is to be done".[22] This involves bringing all parties into face-to-face contact. The second is in terms of a values theory where "restorative justice is anything dealing with restorative values or actions". This would involve all actions leading to "healing rather than hurting".[23] Such reconciliation can only occur after the offence is clearly articulated and the offender, victim and audience are identified in order to be brought together for dialogue in new ways. On a broader social scene, this can be done through bringing together, in dialogue, people from warring or disputing social groupings where injustices have been seen to be done.[24] This process may occur in the organisation in relation to bullying, although the push towards litigation is strong once the "victim" becomes a representative figure for all those as yet unacknowledged acts of bullying. So, ironically, the processes of restoration mean that the roles of bully, victim and organisational/institutional audience become *established* roles for the recurring dramas of fear, guilt, displacement, rage, recrimination, scapegoating and, where possible, eventual reconciliation. This can happen to the extent that those labelled as bullies can themselves become scapegoats and the roles in the drama become interchangeable. In this process, the destructive/creative drama of perversity gets played out at the organisational level.

Second, is the context of how primitive emotions in the workplace are managed. Rage itself is a primitive emotion in the sense that it is one of the very early emotions experienced by the infant. It occurs in response to frustration and can appear so violently that the infant is in danger of choking or losing breath—going blue with rage. The temper tantrums of the toddler are a later expression of rage, often linked to an expressed desire to manipulate the parents, but seemingly taking on a life of their own. Rage is said to overcome us, to blind us, to shake and choke us. It is an expression of intolerable impotence and loss of self-control. It appears when the enraged person is thwarted, disregarded despite their strong desire and, importantly, against their expectation that their desire will be fulfilled. The whole order of the expected universe seems to stand against one and one's usual power of command fails. Rage is a response to a perceived slap in the face. There are other responses, but humiliation followed by rage is one.

Its success and continuation as a fuel for action resides in the fear that rage instils in others. The vengeance motive is to humiliate the other. So rage can work through bullying. Rage begets rage.

Rage may be expressed in a hot and immediate manner—seen in the angry boss who can't get his or her way—or may be tempered and cooled so that it becomes focused in the long term. The effect of the perceived insult that first provoked the rage can shape the long-term goals of vengeance. Revenge cycles and vengeance dynamics are one form of institutionalised rage. Examples of feuds between or within departments are legionary as competition for resources or recognition becomes personalised.

Alternatively, a volatile leader or manager may promote a culture of fear, which may in turn lead to sadistic and masochistic practices unconsciously framed to imitate, appropriate or appease the enraged power. Tyrannical power may institutionalise rage, providing the conditions for further rage to fester. Because tyrannical power is gained through force or is achieved over time through the exploitation and control of others—that is, it is not a form either of democracy or loving authority[25]—it cannot provide the social conditions for alternative responses to frustration, humiliation and loss of control among members of the community. Tyrannical power resides in the fear that it may be overturned, so ever greater control is desired and paranoid mindsets are created. The link between fear and rage is evident in its institutionalised forms.

Anger, the therapists argue, is healthy and far better expressed than turned against the self. But institutionalised anger is another matter. Cultures of bullying, sadism and denigration usually split the organisation. One is either part of the power elite or sycophantic towards it, or one is a victim. There is a great need for more companies to follow the lead of those who consider it important to care for their workforce and overcome the many resistances that systemically work against this. In terms of the armed forces training examples given at the start of this chapter, this means finding whole new attitudes to what defence training means.

Notes

1. From the Investigating Officer's Report into the death of Private Jeremy Williams: *Investigating Officer's Report into the Death of 8299931 Pte. Jeremy Paul Williams Formerly RAINF Initial Employment Trainee School of Infantry, Singleton, 2nd February 2003*, p. 1.
2. Ibid.
3. *The Melbourne Age* newspaper of 4 November 2003 reported this outcome of the 2003 investigation under the headline "Trainee soldiers asked to dob in bullying officers".
4. Ibid.
5. Garrett, J. (2004). "Recent developments in unlawful command influence". *Army Lawyer*, May.
6. Stevens, R. April 2005, WSWS News and Analysis.
7. Posted on the internet by Chamster at http://chamsterswheel. blogspot.com/2006/02/colombias-army-culture-of-sadism.html.
8. See, for example, http://www.bullyonline.org/workbully/military. htm.
9. In WWI, 306 soldiers were executed on the orders of General Haig (known at the time as Butcher Haig) for the sole purpose of instilling fear in the remaining soldiers. It's not recognised that most, and maybe all, the selected soldiers, many of them teenagers, were exhibiting the symptoms of PTSD (Post Traumatic Stress Disorder). Today, General Haig would be regarded as a war criminal but he retains his earldom whilst the families who lost a loved one still bear the shame of false accusations of cowardice and desertion. The Army, and the UK Government, continue to refuse to issue posthumous pardons, presumably because they fear legal action, compensation claims, and closer inspection of unpalatable matters such as continuing deaths in non-combat situations. http://www. bullyonline.org/workbully/military.htm.
10. Klein, M. (1946). "Notes on some schizoid mechanisms". In: J. Mitchell (ed.) *The Selected Melanie Klein*. Harmondsworth: Penguin Books.
11. Bion, W.R. (1961). *Experiences in Groups*. London: Tavistock Publications.
12. Sievers, B. and Mersky, R.R. (2006). "The Economy of Vengeance: Some considerations on the aetiology and meaning of the business of revenge". *Human Relations*, 59 (2): 241–59.
13. Fornari, F. (1966/75). *The Psychoanalysis of War*. Bloomington, IN: University of Indiana press.

14. Sievers, B. and Mersky, R.R. (2006), op. cit., p. 245.
15. Girard, R. (1972). *Violence and the Sacred*. Baltimore, MD: Johns Hopkins University Press.
16. The term accomplice has been used in this book to refer to accomplices in perverse practice at an organisational system level. Sometimes the accomplice may benefit from the practice, as in the case of the board members discussed in Chapter 6. At other times the accomplice may not benefit and may even become victim to the process. While the roles of accomplice and victim are different, the same person or group may move from one role to another during the perverse process. This can happen with high-ranking scapegoats.
17. Freud, S. (1921). *Group Psychology and the Analysis of the Ego*. London: Hogarth Press and the Institute of Psychoanalysis (1949).
18. Bion, W.R. (1961), op. cit.; Sievers, B. and Mersky, R.R. (2006), op. cit.
19. Rayner, C. and Hoel, H. (1997). "A Summary Review of Literature Relating to Workplace Bullying". *Journal of Community and Applied Social Psychology*, 7: 181–91.
20. White, S. (2001). "A life Cycle Theory of Bullying: Persecutory anxiety and a futile search for recognition in the workplace". *Socio-Analysis*, 3 (2): 137–54.
21. Obold-Eshleman, C. (2004). "Victims' Rights and the Danger of Domestication of the Restorative Justice Paradigm". *Notre Dame Journal of Law, Ethics & Public Policy*, 18: 571–603.
22. Ibidem.
23. Ibidem.
24. Bar-On, D. (ed.) (2000). *Bridging the Gap: Storytelling as a way to work through political and collective hostilities*. Hamburg: Koerber-Stiftung.
25. A term used by a participant in a Listening Post discussion in Melbourne, 2007.

CHAPTER EIGHT

The Consumer–Provider Pair

The argument in this book has been to demonstrate the presence of perverse dynamics within organisations and corporations. These dynamics are not simply the result of the presence of perverse individuals, that is, corrupt leaders who would despoil the organisation out of individual greed, pride or envy. There may well be such individuals, although the picture of such localised evil accounts for but a minuscule element of the phenomena described. The dynamics here refer to broader systemic perversity.

The role of a final chapter is normally to help the reader find a positive and hopeful way out from the difficult and rather depressing scenes that have been revealed. For, should not Eros triumph over Thanatos and should not scholarship work towards creative outcomes? The chapter should then address such questions as: How might our corporations become less perverse? How might the more creative and life sustaining forces of organisational life be supported? Moreover, the book has not addressed those impulses within companies and other organisations that reflect appropriate pride, generosity, gratitude and creative endeavour despite the fact that many such instances can be found. But, this was not my intent and there are a plethora of books that provoke the reader to become more creative, work collaboratively and make it more enjoyable, and that demonstrate the positive capacities of success and corporate responsibility.[1] I am intent on exploring perversity within organisations: to know its form and shape before grasping at any quick solution or method of reparation for unintentional ills. There is always attraction in destructivity and its place within and alongside the life forces, if only the attraction of the hope that we might get a better grip on knowing its nature and understanding its insidious grasp; its jouissance as the Lacanians would say.

The case studies have emphasised the destructive nature of collective perversity; have named the excesses of emotion present as corporate sins: perverse pride, greed, envy, sloth and wrath or rage. They have focused on systemic perversity as the domination of narcissistic pleasure over the common good; the concurrent denial and acknowledgement of reality in the turning of a blind eye, and the development of perverse certainty; the engagement of others as perverse accomplices while having a state of mind and promoting the social relation of instrumentality; and, as self-perpetuating in perverse cycles.

There may be times, of course, when the defence of denial is helpful—during extreme pain where there is no realistic escape, for example. The individual frequently pursues his or her own pleasure before that of others. That is not unusual. Narcissism is basic to survival and instrumentalism is a key to survival in some circumstances. We need the group to sustain a human identity and we need others for recognition and a chance to assert ourselves. But, the perverse position, at a social level and in the long run, is counterproductive to human species survival, especially its psychological survival. The collective abuse of others is antithetical to good community.

There are arguments that perversion in itself is a creative social force. These are framed generally within an applied psychoanalysis of the instincts. Brown, for instance, challenges the usual idea of sublimation as the healthy defence.[2] Sublimation, he claims, is not the way out of human neurosis, but simply a redirection of libidinal energies away from the body towards an assumed and invented soul. It is another form of repression of the body. His claim is that we need to return to the body and Eros. Just as the child has a polymorphous perversity, so too should the healthy adult. Repression is the cause of all ills. His argument rests in a line of thinking from the romantics onward. It is found in the idea that freedom from neurosis, repression, guilt, shame and self-loathing might be found in throwing off for ever the binding, imposed responsibilities and restraints of social institutions.

In this tradition, polymorphous perverse tendencies, socially enacted, are described in terms of: (i) individual and collective pleasure beyond the shadow of repressive civilisation; (ii) the transgression of restrictive boundaries and the finding of new vision; and (iii) an unrestrictive relationship with others. Indeed, psychoanalysis as a therapeutic project might (mistakenly) be regarded as having such an aim. As a therapy it is aimed at freeing individuals from the repressive restraints of their own internal aggressors—those institutionalised thoughts that prevent them from finding and acting on their own creative impulses. But, it is not an outright rejection of community.[3]

Indeed, for those examining perverse tendencies in the strictly libidinal terms of erogenous zones, a problem lies in ascertaining the nature and extent of repression required to enable humans to live in healthy relationships without undue restriction leading to neurosis and unhealthy social subjugation. There arises a question of how much polymorphous perversity is normal and sustainable, for the individual and for society.

Bringing in a political dimension, Marcuse introduces the idea of "surplus repression" to distinguish the repressive influence (domination) of social institutions that serve to diminish pleasure, from the "basic repression" required to contain infantile partial sexual impulses.[4] His analysis locates psychic development within a reality principle illuminated by Marxist theory and emphasising the alienation of capitalist labour under conditions of surplus repression. He called this reality principle the "performance principle".

The restrictions upon the libido appear as the more rational, the more universal they become, the more they permeate the whole of society. They operate on the individual as external objective laws and as an internalised force: the societal authority is absorbed into the conscience and into the unconscious of the individual and works as his own desire, morality and fulfillment. In the "normal" development, the individual lives his repression "freely" as his own life: he desires what he is supposed to desire; his gratifications are profitable to him and to others; he is reasonably and even often exuberantly happy. This happiness . . . allows him to continue his performance . . . and, in so doing reproduces more or less adequately society as a whole.[5]

Such a distinction provides some differentiation of perverse tendencies from the simple unrepressed and free expression of libido. That is, it provides for an acceptable normality. After Marcuse, the unrepressed need no longer necessarily be perverse. On the contrary, it may consist of those natural life forces that are dominated by what might now (in terms of the current book) be seen as a perverse institution, developed through the effects of surplus repression. More than in Brown's analysis, Marcuse locates the struggle between life and death forces clearly in the nature of social institutions.

Along with others who were reading Freud from a more socially radical perspective[6] this formed a line of thinking that helped buoy up the transformations of the 1960s in the west: women's liberation, the sexual revolution, racial, political emancipation and, later, gay rights. Ironically, however, the social movements so sustained have now also contributed to the opposing ideologies of the neo-conservatists, individualism, free markets and rapid increases in consumerism and commodification of values, because they have freed many previously dominated groups to join institutionalised capitalism through its now narcissistic and individualised form, embracing and guiding them into the performance principle and its twin principle of consumerism.

Despite the Marxist Freudians of the mid-twentieth century, a view of freedom as the removal of repression from dominating institutions unfortunately confused the dynamics of the inner psychology of the person (where oedipal authority reigns) with a systems or socio-analysis of the organisation (where what Lawrence calls the "sphinx" reigns).[7] It posited an idealistic notion that a free Eros might overcome institutional domination as if: (a) Eros belongs to the individual and never to the collective as a whole, and (b) destructivity were not an essential part of life to be negotiated through the building of relationship. The lifting of (inner) repression by itself was a goal, framed within the therapeutic psychoanalytic project. But, this approach does not take into account the social systems aspect of applied psychoanalytic thinking. What kind of social analysis is required now in the twenty-first century?

Psychoanalysis as a probe into social being goes beyond the individual therapeutic aim. The organisation or corporation is not just individual writ large; not just a person with neuroses or psychoses. Even though the system seems, at times, to display such tendencies because it shares with the individual (system) dynamics such as splitting, projection, denial and negation, this is because both individual and organisation share the fundamentals of human system dynamics that are located in culture.[8] We have thus far discovered something of the perverse emotional life of the organisation in following the prompt to think of it "as if" it were a person. But, a therapeutic approach, developed as it has been on the psychology of the individual, will not do. The organisation is a collectivity, created through a process of social agreements, both consciously formulated and unconsciously influenced. If it has a character, it is not one that can become sick and might be cured—at least not in the sense derived from the medical paradigm. It is a social character that is formed through contracts, negotiations, rules, agreements, unconscious collusions and political co-relations. Its "health" is dependent upon adequate communication, good authority, clear role relations and ethical process. Psychoanalysis as a social, rather than individual probe can explore the unconscious underworld of these contracts and agreements; these pacts among sub-groupings and the dynamics that form the glue between sub-system parts. It can explore those social defences that operate to defend organisation members against the intolerable aspects of their tasks or against unwanted emotions in the work culture.

Whole-of-society dynamics operate to create and maintain social institutions. Implicit, tacit and unconscious agreements create, undo and recreate our social worlds, their pasts, present and futures. We can examine inter-subjective alliances, pacts and contracts found in the "social ensembles of family, group and institution".[9] These form and maintain unconsciousness. A series of systems of agreements can be discerned as developed and supported through unconscious collusions. The unconscious is not simply a place in the mind of an individual, but a web of social relations. Unconscious fantasy is a social phenomenon, shared within group dynamics and internalised by individuals.[10] It exists in a network or matrix and may be discovered through cultural products such as dreams[11] or group formations.[12]

This book has looked at the organisation "as if" it were an individual, finding that the dynamics of the whole operate with a systems (if not a moral) integrity of their own. But, more to the point, we should regard the individual "as if" he or she were an organisation writ small. If we understand the system dynamics as shared; as the basis of the operating metaphor, then the social system or network of meaning might be primary and the individual who internalises this system, secondary. And, if unconsciousness is found in the ensemble or the network—the mental matrix[13] or Symbolic order[14]—perverse organisational dynamics must be understood as operating through this unconsciousness. Moreover, the organisation sits within a broader society that shapes its rules, agreements and unconscious social pacts. The question then arises: what is the dominant tenor of our current culture? What is the fulcrum within which the organisational and corporate character is forged?

The Consumer Society[15]

In Chapter 2, Freud's analysis of fetishism was described as prototypical of the perverse dynamic.[16] The fetish is a veil or substitute for the object of desire. It is a symbol of lust for the object; a primitive link to the other. In social anthropology the idea of the fetish has long been associated with rites in primitive religions and associated with the power of the phallus. Whether regarded as an object of sublimated desire, or as entwined with religious ecstasy, the fetish is a symbol of irrational and perverse desire, having no value in itself yet having the power to sustain that desire.

The notion of *commodity fetishism* places the dynamic of fetishism broadly into the analysis of market dynamics.[17] The commodification of our social lives is created through market dynamics, where objects become valued not for their use, but for a symbolic exchange-value. The fact that, for example, gold is more highly valued than immediately useful objects leads to the idea of its being a fetish. Its value is fetishistic rather than intrinsic. In this world, people also become commodities whose labour is bought and sold and whose direct social relations become modified by their place in the market. Commodities and market relations become the fetishistic expression of direct human relations that themselves become lost. Consumerism then becomes a central and necessary organising principle in a world of commodities.

The institutional containers of consumerism change over time. The twentieth century gradually grew away from institutionalised bureacracy, with its social assumptions of dependency, towards an organisational form of individualism. Increasingly aware of the need to drag ourselves away from closed and insular forms of organisational life, and projected headlong towards the twenty-first century by sophisticated technology, western society and, increasingly, the so-called third world, rediscovered the customer and the producer/consumer pair.

Although consumerism as a fully developed organising principle for social life has a history that goes back at least to the Industrial Revolution, a renewed focus on the customer has become apparent in work organisations.[18] The post-modern era is heavily invested in service industries, and the thinking within service industries has permeated other industry sectors with its customer emphasis. Moreover, the new customer is not unsophisticated. She is likely to represent a section within a large company with its own economic power, or a client of a government service well aware of her rights. Nor are enterprise relations with that customer simple. Best practice involves a relationship that is mutually co-operative, where producer and customer work collaboratively to discover customer requirements in the context of their broader situation.

The relatedness of each consumer–provider pair seems, at first sight, to centre on rational economic exchange and informed customer service.[19] For example, Du Gay and Salaman argue that a new "discourse of the enterprise" has come into being where the customer becomes "sovereign" because of an enterprise reframing in response to a market economy.[20] The customer-producer paradigm has restructured work, changed work practices, shifted authority for production to the consumer and, most significantly, re-shaped the notion of self within organisations.[21]

However, this seemingly rational exchange, albeit fuelled through ideological manipulation and tacitly enacted in social process, covers a deeper picture. If the very nature of self within organisations has changed, that change has been via the development of a narcissistic false self. Hoggett examines this in terms of Arlie Hochschild's notion of "deep acting" where members become strongly identified with the organisation to the extent that their organisational role, with its attendant beliefs and attitudes, takes over the character of the role holder.[22] No longer simply acting *in* a role, their experience is deeply *of* the role. They become more fully part of the organisation due to increasing demands that the employee genuinely take on the values of the organisation and show this to the outside world. Such demands have their benefits and costs. Appearing to be more fully communal through close identification, this appearance is in fact an illusion, albeit at times a deeply held and convincing illusion.

The illusion of communality is the partner illusion to the idea of the unattached individual. Here, a form of false self is the result of a narcissistic social defence where the individual withdraws from authentic communal life (subject to subject) and takes an instrumental attitude to his or her work organisation. In brief my argument is as follows.[23]

1. Consumerism involves the simplification of roles and their associated tasks, and in so doing fundamentally changes the relation of the subject to the group and the institution. Consumerism as a central or dominant value leads to many complex organisational and societal roles being collapsed under the more dominant role of consumer. This is seen when roles such as "patient", meaning "one who suffers"; or "student", meaning "one who studies and learns"; or "citizen", meaning "member of a state", are all named as "customers". Moreover, the re-signification of roles in a consumer society results in the potential and actual loss of learning from the experience that is inherent in the richer role of patient, student or citizen. This role change also affects the doctors, teachers and governments who are their role counterparts. Do these latter simply (in parallel) become "providers" or "suppliers" and what might this mean? As a corollary to this, the social institutions linked to the submerged or lost role aspects, are themselves minimised or submerged. The shadow of the submerged aspect lies in the consumer role in a repressed fashion and may engender frustration and rage at their loss.

2. Consumerism is a social dynamic related to the individual dynamic of secondary narcissism, classically conceptualised.[24] Both involve a focus on the ego or self—e.g., the customer is always right. Both are concerned with the fulfilment of a desire that has been shaped, if not initially created, within the social field. Moreover, Freud's conceptualisation of secondary narcissism clearly argues that the withdrawal of libidinal interest from the "other" onto the "ego" (object-libido transformed into ego-libido)[25] concerns a change in the relation of the subject to reality. Actual complexities are disavowed in favour of monolithic world views or delusions.[26] The same might

be said of the consumer's relation to the institution. As argued above, the collapse of complex roles into mono-dimensional consumer roles constitutes an altered state of role relations; mostly sustained by a delusional advertising industry.

3. During times of rapid change, alongside the breakdown of many institutional values comes an increase in uncertainty and anxiety, a questioning of identity, disenchantment and pain. In our work organisations, such transformations have, in recent years, led to a narcissistic defence against these feelings. This is evidenced psychologically through isolation, withdrawal, instrumental attitudes to work and a sense of "beating the system" before it beats you.[27] Importantly, a societal defence against the pain and anomie has grown. It is a defence that seems on the surface to favour autonomy, however, on closer examination this can be seen as "individualism" with little accountability to the group: a false deluded individualism because of its slavish devotion to the corporation rather than to a really democratic collective.[28] Such a narcissistic defence is one that comes with the human cost of loss of self-reliance, creativity and learning.[29] It paradoxically destroys a more creative individual autonomy; one that derives from responsible group membership where personal authority can grow. The cost to the group is that it becomes a pseudo-group rather than a psychologically meaningful group.

4. Alongside the narcissistic defence, socially evidenced in consumerism, is the economic rationalist argument. This is itself defensive, but constructed as a conscious rationale for sustaining an individualist position for the subject. Economic rationalism is a philosophy, like consumerism, that is instrumental. In its climate, a new managerialism has grown with the imperative to save/make money. This has led, in many situations, to submerging the intrinsic value of the work done within our organisations.

If, in the consumer society, the self has been transformed towards greater narcissism and individuality; institutions have become founded on the consumer–provider pair. It is this role relation that provides the dominant ensemble for the unconscious fantasy of the organisation. It has been placed over the employer–employee relation and the manager–subordinate relation which still exist but lie beneath the mask (presented to the outside world) of collaborative, team-based corporations. This is a major fantasy that structures organisational life and reaches even into the non-corporate forms of organisation.

The Consumer–Provider Pair

The values of consumerism are linked to a view (fantasy) of the independent individual rather than the community. However, on the evidence of psychoanalysis, or even general social psychology, this individual is in many senses a myth.[30] More likely, the subject he or she appears to be is either a person separated from the community in a withdrawn and counter-dependent manner, or one who does not recognise the essential relatedness that embeds them. That is, one who is linked through the role of "provider" or "consumer" in a limited relation of perceived, yet illusory, mutual advantage, rather than through a plethora of relations grounded in additional moral bases, such as provided through values of loyalty, devotion, care etc. Community relations under such an ideology become economic and instrumental rather than developed through shared work where trust is established by means of mutual experience. Objects and activities within communities and organisations become fetishes.

"Because employment is perceived as being increasingly unreliable, and the 'organisation' is no longer a safe container and provider of institutional defences against anxiety, we are seeing a widespread phenomenon of psychological withdrawal. Instead of dependency, the individual has adopted a much more instrumental relationship."[31] Growing globalisation and uncertainty about the future leaves people in a vulnerable state in their work organisations. Rather than working through their very real dependencies, many have drawn back to a pseudo-independence aided by the ideologies of the predominant enterprise/consumer discourse. Yet we are at a time in history when interdependence is critical. John Bowlby's theory of attachment is relevant.[32] When a child is attached to an important other, say the mother, lengthy separation results in three stages—protest, withdrawal and finally pseudo adaptation where the child develops a mistrusting and detached attitude which is hidden by a superficial mode of being in relationships. The final adaptation is fundamentally instrumental and is in response to perceived abandonment.

Is this a picture that fits twenty-first-century western societies? Have modern citizens been traumatically separated from those institutions that once were dependable rather than being weaned from them through a process of increasing maturity? This is the state-of-being of a consumer society: a state of instrumentality and superficial relationship hiding a deeper fear of uncertainty about unresolved dependence. The ideas that we are all independent consumers, that the market is wise, that government should simply legislate rather than be a direct public service; these ideas, through their dominant enactment, may literally be uncontainable in traditional institutions with their eroded traditional values. Citizens lose faith in their governments. Some, unable to tolerate the uncertainty, return to the traditional roots of fundamental religion, others turn to addictions of various sorts.

What then might be the new container for these thoughts and this state of mind? Is the consumer–provider pair acting as a transitional container that may lead to a more creative social arrangement? Is this state of mind leading us towards the condition of freedom from repression, heralded in the 1950s? Or does it denote the new values and a social defensive relation that is based on the primarily economic and instrumental position of mutual perceived advantage which may stand in opposition to values such as loyalty, mature representation and interdependence (themselves based on identificatory relations with an institution over and above instrumental interpersonal relations)? Is it consistent with narcissistic individual and social defences against anxiety—especially in the face of declining institutional values? Such is the permissive yet still dominating twenty-first-century super-ego insofar as it paves the way for the perverse state of mind: the subject's denial of recognition of his or her place in the social order.

The superego has but one imperative: "obey!", which today is translated as "Jois!", otherwise translated as "Shop!" Of course the superego not only enjoins you to shop, but to enjoy doing it; you must be glad to obey the order, even though this order is presented as a free choice.[33]

No longer is the defence simply against unresolved dependence. It is a response to abandonment; a deep rift between the individual self and the social institution. The elements of systemic perversity that have been outlined in this book—namely, narcissistic pleasure over the common good; the concurrent denial and acknowledgement of reality in the turning of a blind eye; the engagement of others as perverse accomplices while having a state of mind and promoting the social relation of instrumentality; and as self-perpetuating in perverse cycles, are institutional outgrowths of the narcissistic society dominated by the consumer–provider pair. In this, consumerism cannot be satisfied. It is the modern embodiment of desire—a state always at odds with restraint.

Members of a Listening Post in Melbourne, January 2007 developed the hypothesis that the new behaviours demanded of citizens by the realisation that global warming is a reality no longer able to be denied, required humans to find new identities. New ways of thinking and approaching life are needed. This in turn requires new social containers. In the discussion, there was a sense that individual citizens, given support, education and collective action were able to banish their denial of the impending problems of climate change and the associated problems of untrammelled consumerism and accept the reality. But, many corporations and governments were seen as unable to do this.[34] Their current existence was based on denial.

There exists a split between individuals as citizens and work organisations. Too often people feel one set of desires and hold one set of values as citizens and another in their organisational or corporate roles. This is not simply because they are hypocrites, although the internal conflicts aroused may give rise to this interpretation of their experience. It is because the work organisation and the private individual are subject to different unconscious networks at war with one another; currently split off from one another. If some organisations become perverse, then it may be because they are the sites where rigid certainty, instrumentality and perverse practice are unconsciously projected. We all love to hate a bad "corporate" as the Australian film *The Bank* demonstrated.[35] But if the corporation is only seen as bad, then there is little chance for the split to be healed.

Is there an institutional container that can hold this split? The old institutions have not held. Even though, as Marcuse said, capitalism provides for a more or less adequate, albeit alienated society, the split gets larger. What might a new container be?

A challenge for the future will be to contextualise the consumer–provider pair in an identificatory dynamic with issues and values *beyond* that pair (for example, issues of environment, quality of life, especially for the disadvantaged, and education). This must be done through a process that brings back lost checks and balances to organisational life. This requires healthy restraint and the recognition and development of closer interdependencies between us all. It means that the perverse dynamics currently operating in so many organisations are understood and constructively ameliorated.

While not being in active pursuit of a solution to the problem of the perverse organisation, perhaps this should be said:

1. that the corporatised form that has coloured, if not infected the twenty-first-century organisation needs to find a new morality and a richer set of roles than the instrumental uni-dimensional providers and consumers that it currently has; and,

2. that the perverse tendencies of some corporations can only be addressed when the split between individual (as person and as citizen) and organisation (with people in corporate roles) is in meaningful dialogue. This can only be achieved in a transparent and regulated environment, and only with the recognition that the forces involved are largely unconscious social processes.

To seek out and prosecute corrupt individuals is important, but akin to catching the street drug dealer rather than the international trafficker. Ken Lay of Enron, Ray Williams of HIH and Calisto Tanzi of Parmalat all suffered from pride and greed. This led them, along with others, into corruption. We need not see them as personally perverse. In many ways they see themselves as righteously attempting to uphold companies that should have flourished. Nonetheless, the perversity was in the cultures surrounding them and their behaviours were sustained by those cultures. Their cover-ups were often acts of desperation as the companies in which they believed, towards which they held an attitude of vehement certainty in regard to their success, began to crumble. Certainly these men had a central role to play and, to the extent that they made deliberate and criminal choices that damaged others, they are accountable. But, leaders are as much products of their groups as the groups are of them, and often they are the products of the unrecognised and unconscious impulses of the group.

"Who needs me?" is a question of character which suffers a radical challenge in modern capitalism. The system radiates indifference. It does so in terms of the outcomes of human striving . . . It radiates indifference in the organisation of absence and trust, where there is no reason to be needed. And it does so through reengineering of institutions in which people are treated as disposable. Such practices obviously and brutally diminish the sense of mattering as a person, of being necessary to others.[36]

In perverse culture, the other is needed only in terms of being an object, a slave or commodity. This includes the accomplice. What's more, it doesn't necessarily feel bad. This is the seduction: if you keep your job and save some income, as a modern day consumer slave you can enjoy yourself and also turn a blind eye. There is something in it for all parties. But, for how long?

To expand beyond the narrow consumer–provider pair means change for all. It means that we must have the social means of stepping aside from personal interests and for examining our collective processes. It also means finding new ways of relating to each other at work. The hope is that some companies may, and do, genuinely attempt this.

In Closing

This book has examined the idea that organisations may be structured as perverse systems, according to five criteria of perversity. In the book, I suggest that in finding evidence of perversity in organisations, this might provide evidence of a perverse structure in society. In this argument, I do not imply that only the perverse structure exists. There are many underlying social-psychological structures in society and in the groups that compose it and these have existed since human culture began. The perverse structure is just one. Its modern day expression has been discussed and one lesson from this book is that it is wise to learn about it. When it is operating in an organisation it may take the form of one of the damaging "deadly organisational sins". Through exploring the presence and form of organisational perversity, we can come to understand its dynamics and effects on people and learn how better to avoid the damage it may cause.

Notes

1. See, for example, Collins, J.C. and Porras, J.I. (1994). *Built to Last: Successful habits of visionary companies.* NY: Harper Collins; and Rosenbluth, H. and McFerrin Peters, D. (1998). *In Good Company: Caring as fiercely as you compete: Lessons from America's best companies.* Addison-Wesley.
2. Brown, N.O. (1959). *Life Against Death: The psychoanalytic meaning of history.* Middletown, CT: Wesleyan University Press.
3. Benjamin, J. (1988). *The Bonds of Love.* NY: Pantheon Books.
4. Marcuse, H. (1955). *Eros and Civilization.* London: Sphere Books.
5. Ibid., p. 51.
6. Robinson, P. (1969). *The Freudian Left: Wilhelm Reich, Geza Roheim, Herbert Marcuse.* NY: Harper and Row.
7. Lawrence, W.G. (1999). "Centring of the Sphinx for the Psycho-analytic Study of Organisations". *Socio-Analysis,* 1 (2): 99–126.
8. Long, S. (1992). *A Structural Analysis of Small Groups.* London: Routledge.
9. Kaes, R. (2002). "Contributions from France: psychoanalysis and institutions in France". In: Robert D. Hinshelwood and Marco Chiesa (eds) *Organizations, Anxieties and Defences: Toward a psychoanalytic social psychology.* London: Whurr Publishers.
10. Puget, J. (2002). "Contributions from South America: from the group as jig-saw puzzle to the incomplete whole". In: Robert D. Hinshelwood and Marco Chiesa (eds) *Organizations, Anxieties and Defences: Toward a psychoanalytic social psychology.* London: Whurr Publishers.
11. Lawrence, W.G. (1998). "Won from the void and formless infinite". In: W.G. Lawrence (ed.) *Social Dreaming @ Work.* London: Karnac Books; Lawrence, W.G. (2005). *Introduction to Social Dreaming: Transforming thinking.* London: Karnac.
12. Foulkes, S.H. *Therapeutic Group Analysis.* NY: International Universities Press.
13. Lawrence, W.G. (1998), op. cit.; Lawrence, W.G. (2000). *Tongued with Fire: Groups in experience.* London: Karnac Books.

14. Lacan, J. (1977). *Ecrits*. London: Tavistock Publications.
15. A prior version of this section was published in Long, S. (1999). "The Tyranny of the Customer and the Cost of Consumerism: An analysis using systems and psycho-analytic approaches to groups and society". *Human Relations*, 52 (6): 723–44.
16. Wastell, D. (1996) gives an analysis of technique in information systems development as a fetishistic practice.
17. Marx, *Capital: A critique of political economy*. In three volumes edited by Fredrick Engles. Chicago, IL: Charles H. Kerr and Co.
18. McKendrick, N., Brewer, J. and Plumb, J.H. (1983). *The Birth of a Consumer Society*. London: Hutchinson; Knights, D. and Morgan, G. (1993). "Organization Theory and Consumption in a Post-Modern Era". *Organization Studies*, 14 (2): 211–34.
19. Knights, D. and Morgan, G. (1993), op. cit.
20. Du Gay, P. and Salaman, G. (1992). "The Cult[ure] of the Customer". *Journal of Management Studies*, 29 (5): 615–33. These authors draw on a range of perspectives in developing this idea of the discourse of the enterprise. For example, Foucault, M. (1979). "On Governmentality". *Ideology and Consciousness*, 6: 5–21. Abercrombie, N. (1991). "The privilege of the producer". In: R. Keat and N. Abercrombie (eds) *Enterprise Culture*. London: Routledge, pp. 171–85. Peters, T. and Waterman, R. (1982). *In Search of Excellence*. New York: Harper and Row. Rose, N. (1990). *Governing the Soul*. London: Routledge.
21. Ibid.
22. Hoggett, P. (2002). "Putting Emotion to Work in the Feeling State". *Socio-Analysis*, 4: 15–32.
23. These ideas are developed more fully in Long, S. (1999), op. cit.
24. Freud, S. (1914). "On narcissism: an introduction". *SE*, 14: 73–102. London: Hogarth Press, 1957.
25. Ibid., p. 75.
26. Freud, S. (1924). "Loss of reality in neurosis and psychosis". *SE*, 19: 183–90. London: Hogarth Press, 1957.
27. Miller, E.J. (1993). *The Vicissitudes of Identity*. Opening Address to the 3rd International Group Relations and Scientific Conference, Lorne, Victoria, Australia.
28. Ralston Saul, J. (1997). *The Unconscious Civilization*. Harmondsworth: Penguin Books.
29. See Bowlby, J. (1988). *A Secure Base: Clinical applications of attachment theory*. London: Routledge, for a discussion about the growth of self-reliance and the interpersonal conditions that sustain it.

30. Sullivan, H.S. (1950). "The Illusion of Personal Individuality". *Psychiatry*, 13: 317–32; Lacan, J. (1977), op. cit.
31. Miller, E.J. (1995). "The healthy organization for the 1990s". In: S. Long (ed.) *International Perspectives on Organizations in Times of Turbulence*. Melbourne: Swinburne University publication.
32. Bowlby, J. (1988), op. cit.
33. Pope, R. (2006). *Cultural Psychoanalysis, or Theory, Resurrected.* http://muse.jhu.edu/journals/theory_and_event/v009/9.1pope.html.
34. This is not to deny those corporations that are attempting to take on a socially responsible role. The idea followed here is that in the current social conditions and due to the imperative of shareholder gain, this requires special dedication.
35. In this film a farmer, whose farm is being reclaimed by the bank that holds its unpaid mortgage, is seen in gradually increasing anguish as his and his family's financial plight deepens and their lives become destroyed. His several attempts to remain in dialogue with the bank officials come to naught. His mounting anger comes to climax as he takes a rifle into the bank. When I saw the film, the audience stood up and cheered at this point. The bank was depicted as an uncaring, distant and ruthless institution. An object at which to direct hate.
36. Sennett, R. (1998). *The Corrosion of Character: The personal consequences of work in the new capitalism.* NY: W.W. Norton and Company, p. 146.

REFERENCES

Abercrombie, N. (1991). "The privilege of the producer". In: R. Keat and N. Abercrombie (eds) *Enterprise Culture*. London: Routledge, pp. 171–85.

Adler, A. (1912). *"The Neurotic Character"*. In: *The Collected Clinical Works of Alfred Adler, Volume 1* (2003), Alfred Adler Institute of Northwestern Washington.

Adler, A. (1998). *Social Interest* (revised edition). London: Oneworld publications.

Armstrong, D. (1995). "The Analytic Object in Organisational Work". Paper delivered at the *Symposium of the International Society for the Psychoanalytic Study of Organisations*. London, July, 1995.

Bain, A. (1994). "Organizational Life Today: Five Hypotheses". Paper presented to *The Australian Institute of Social Analysis Seminar Day*, Melbourne, 2 July, 1994.

Bain, A. (1999). "On Socio-Analysis". *Socio-Analysis*, 1 (1): 1–21.

Bain, A., Long, S. and Ross, S. (1992). *Paper Houses: The authority vacuum in a government school*. Melbourne: Collins Dove.

Bakan, J. (2004). *The Corporation: The pathological pursuit of profit and power*. London: Constable.

Ballantyne, T. (2002). *"What Really went Wrong at Ansett?"* www. spiritsofansett.com/history/ballantyne.htm.

Bar-On, D. (ed.) *Bridging the Gap: Storytelling as a way to work through political and collective hostilities*. Hamburg: Koerber-Stiftung.

Benjamin, J. (1988). *The Bonds of Love*. NY: Pantheon Books.

Benjamin, J. (1995). *Like Subjects, Love Objects: Essays on recognition and sexual difference*. New Haven, CT: Yale University Press.

166

Benvenuto, S. (2006). "Perversion and charity: an ethical approach". In: D. Nobus and L. Downing (eds) (2006). *Perversion: Psychoanalytic perspectives*, pp. 59–78. London: Karnac.

Bion, W.R. (1961). *Experiences in Groups*. London: Tavistock Publications.

Bion, W.R. (1962). *Learning From Experience*. London: Karnac, 1984.

Bion, W.R. (1967). *Second Thoughts*. London: Karnac Books.

Bion, W.R. (1970). *Attention and Interpretation*. London: Tavistock Publications.

Bion, W.R. (1975). *Brazilian Lectures*. London: Karnac Books, 1990.

Bowlby, J. (1988). *A Secure Base: Clinical applications of attachment theory.* London: Routledge.

Brimelow, J. (2004). *Review of "When Genius Failed" by Robert Lowenstein.* www.vdare.com/jb/ltcm.htm.

Brown, N.O. (1959). *Life Against Death: The psychoanalytic meaning of history.* Middletown, CT: Wesleyan University Press.

Business Week Special Report *The Best and Worst Boards* 7 October 2002.

Chancellor, E. (2002). "Perverse Incentives". *The Australian Financial Review,* 7 June.

Chapman, J. (1992). "Basic Assumption Subjunctive". *Australian Institute of Social Analysis Newsletter,* No. 1. 1993.

Chapman, J. (1999). "Hatred and Corruption of Task". *Socio-Analysis,* 1 (2): 127–50.

Chattopadhyay, G. (1995). "Hierarchy and Modern Organisation". In: S. Long (ed.) *International Perspectives on Organizations in Times of Turbulence.* Melbourne: Swinburne University publication.

Chasseguet-Smirgel, J. (1984). *Creativity and Perversion*. London: Free Association Books.

Collins, J.C. and Porras, J.I. (1994). *Built to Last: Successful habits of visionary companies.* NY: Harper Collins.

Creese, E. (1995). "The Balance of Arts and Management Cultures". In: Performing Arts Organizations. Paper delivered at the Monash, Deakin and Swinburne University of Technology joint seminar, Royal Park Hospital.

Dalgleish, J. and Long, S. (2006). "Management's fear of market demands: a psychodynamic exploration". In: E. Klein and I.L. Pritchard (eds) *Relatedness in a Global Economy*, pp. 101–23. London: Karnac.

Deleuze, G. and Guattari, F. (1983). *Anti-Oedipus: Capitalism and schizophrenia.* St Paul, MN: University of Minnesota.

Derrida, J. (1997). Politics and Friendship: A discussion with Jacques Derrida. Center for Modern French Thought, University of Sussex, 1 December 1997.

Downing, L. (2006). "Perversion, historicity, ethics". In: D. Nobus and L. Downing (eds) (2006). *Perversion: Psychoanalytic perspectives*, pp. 149–64. London: Karnac.

Du Gay, P. and Salaman, G. (1992). "The Cult[ure] of the Customer". *Journal of Management Studies*, 29 (5): 615–33.

Dunbar, N. (2001). *Inventing Money: The story of Long-Term Capital Management and the legends behind it.* NY: John Wiley and Sons.

Eisold, K. (2003). Corrupt Groups in Contemporary Corporations: Outside boards and inside traders. Paper given at the *ISPSO Symposium 'Power and Politics in Organizations'*, Boston.

Eisold, K. (1998). "The Splitting of the New York Psychoanalytic Society and the Construction of Psychoanalytic Authority". *The International Journal of Psycho-Analysis* (October), 79 (5): 871–85.

Eisold, K. (1994). "The Intolerance of Diversity in Psychoanalytic Institutes". *Journal of Applied Psychoanalysis*, 75: 785–800.

Emery, F.E. and Trist, E.L. (1965). "The Causal Texture of Organization Environments". *Human Relations*, 18: 21–32.

Erikson, E.H. (1950). *Childhood and Society.* London and NY: W.W. Norton.

Fink, B. (1995). *The Lacanian Subject: Between language and jouissance.* Princeton, NJ: Princeton University Press.

Flynn, R. "Impediments to Organisational Effectiveness—social defences and shame in the workplace". *Socio-Analysis*, 3 (2): 109–22.

Fornari, F. (1966/75). *The Psychoanalysis of War.* Bloomington, IN: University of Indiana Press.

Foucault, M. (1963). *Madness and Civilization: A history of insanity in the age of reason.* NY: Random House.

Foucault, M. (1979). "On Governmentality". *Ideology and Consciousness*, 6: 5–21.

Foucault, M. (2003). *Abnormal: Lectures at the College de France 1974–75.* London: Verso.

Foulkes, S.H. *Therapeutic Group Analysis.* NY: International Universities Press.

Fraher, A. (2004). *A History of Group Study and Psychodynamic Organizations.* NY: Free Association Books.

Freire, P. (1970). *Pedogogy of the Oppressed.* London: Penguin Books.

Freud, S. (1900). *The Interpretation of Dreams.* Edited by James Strachey and revised by Angela Richards, The Pelican Freud Library, Harmondsworth: Penguin Books, 1976.

Freud, S. Three Essays on the Theory of Sexuality (1905). In: *Sigmund Freud: On Sexuality.* Harmondsworth: Penguin, 1977, pp. 31–169.

Freud, S. (1913). *Totem and Taboo*. London: Routledge and Kegan Paul 1960.

Freud, S. (1914). "On Narcissism: An introduction". *SE*, 14: 73–102. London: Hogarth Press, 1957.

Freud, S. (1924). "Loss of Reality in Neurosis and Psychosis". *SE*, 19: 183–90. London: Hogarth Press, 1957.

Freud, S. (1927). "Fetishism". *SE*, 21. London: Hogarth Press, 1978.

Freud, S. (1921). *Group Psychology and the Analysis of the Ego*. London: Hogarth Press and the Institute of Psychoanalysis (1949).

Freud, S. (1940). "Splitting of the Ego in the Process of Defence". In: *Sigmund Freud: On Metapsychology and the Theory of Psychoanalysis*. Harmondsworth: Penguin Books, 1984.

Fusaro, P. and Miller, R. (2002). *What Went Wrong at Enron: Everyone's guide to the largest bankruptcy in US history*. USA: Wiley and Sons.

Garrett, J. (2004). Recent developments in unlawful command influence. *Army Lawyer*, May.

Gettler, L. (2005). *Organisations Behaving Badly: A Greek tragedy of corporate pathology*. Queensland: Wiley.

Giddens, A. (1990). *The Consequences of Modernity*. Oxford: Blackwell, 1991.

Gillin, L. and Long, S. (2004). "Integration of Psychosocial Theory". Paper delivered at the Conference of *Small Enterprise Association of Australia and New Zealand*, Brisbane.

Girard, R. (1972). *Violence and the Sacred*. Baltimore, MD: Johns Hopkins University Press.

Goldberg, A. (2006). "An overview of perverse behaviour". In: D. Nobus and L. Downing (eds) (2006). *Perversion: Psychoanalytic perspectives*, pp. 39–58. London: Karnac.

Gordon, M. (2006). "A Democracy to Come: First the small group and then the world (Some reflections on Derrida's concept of Democracy to come)". Unpublished paper.

Gottliebsen (2003). *10 Best and 10 Worst Decisions of Australian CEOs 1992–2002*. Camberwell, Australia: Viking, Penguin Group.

Gould, L.J., Stapley, L.F. and Stein, M. (2001). *The Systems Psychodynamics of Organizations: Integrating the group relations approach, psychoanalytic, and open systems perspectives*. London: H. Karnac (Books) Limited.

Gould, L.J., Stapley, L.F. and Stein, M. (2004a). *Experiential Learning in Organizations: Applications of the Tavistock Group Relations Approach*. London: Karnac Books Ltd.

Gould, L., Stapley, L. and Stein, M. (2004b). *Systems Psychodynamics*. London: Karnac.

Grotstein, J.S. (1981). "Wilfred Bion: the man, the psychoanalyst, the mystic. A perspective on his life and work." In: J.S. Grotstein (ed.) *Do I Dare Disturb the Universe?: A memorial to Wilfred R. Bion.* London: Caesura Press.

Hamilton, V. (1982). *Narcissus and Oedipus: The children of psychoanalysis.* London, Boston: Routledge and Kegan Paul.

Harré, R. (1984). "Social Elements as Mind". *British Journal of Medical Psychology,* 57: 127–35.

Hegel, G.W.F. (1998). *Phenomenology of Spirit.* In: S. Houlgate (ed.) *The Hegel Reader.* Oxford: Blackwell Publishers.

Hinshelwood, R.D. (1991). *A Dictionary of Kleinian Thought.* London: Free Association Books.

Hirschhorn, L. (1988). *The Workplace Within: Psychodynamics of organizational life.* Cambridge, MA: MIT Press.

Hoggett, P. (1992). *Partisans in an Uncertain World: The psychoanalysis of engagement.* London: Free Association Books.

Hoggett, P. (2002). "Putting Emotion to Work". In: "The Feeling State". *Socio-Analysis,* 4: 15–32.

Hoggett, P. (2006). Review of the "Unconscious at Work", edited by Obholtzer and Roberts in *Free Associations.*

Hoggett, P., Mayo, M. and Miller, C. (2006). "On Good Authority". *Socio-Analysis,* 8: 1–16.

Hunt, J.M. "Organisational Leadership and Shame". www.ispso.org/Symposia/London/2000hunt.htm.

Janis, I.L. (1986). *Victims of Groupthink: A psychological study of foreign policy decisions and fiascos.* Boston, MA: Houghton Mifflin.

Jaques, E. (1955). "Social systems as a defense against persecutory and depressive anxiety". In: M. Klein, P. Heimann and R. Money-Kyrle (eds) *New Directions in Psychoanalysis.* London: Tavistock Publications.

Jaques, E. (1989). *Requisite Organization: The CEO's guide to creative structure and leadership.* USA: Carson Hall and Co.

Kaes, R. (2002). "Contributions from France: psychoanalysis and institutions in France". In: R.D. Hinshelwood and M. Chiesa (eds) *Organizations, Anxieties and Defences: Toward a psychoanalytic social psychology.* London: Whurr Publishers.

Karpin, D. (1995). *Enterprising Nation: Renewing Australia's Managers to Meet the Challenges of the Asia-Pacific Century.* Report of the Industry Task Force on Leadership and Management Skills, Australian Government Printer.

Kernberg, Otto J. (1996). "Thirty Methods to Destroy the Creativity of Psychoanalytic Candidates". *International Journal of Psycho-Analysis,* 77 (5): 1031–40.

Kernberg, O. (2006). "Perversion, perversity and normality: diagnostic and therapeutic considerations". In: D. Nobus and L. Downing (eds) *Perversion: Psychoanalytic perspectives*, pp. 19–38. London: Karnac.

Kets de Vries, M. (1999). "What's Playing in the Organizational Theatre? Collusive relationships in management." *Human Relations*, 52 (6): 745–74.

Kirsner, D. (1999). "Life among the analysts". *Free Associations*, 17 (43).

Kirsner, D. (2000). *Unfree Associations: Inside Psychoanalytic Institutes*. NY: Other Press.

Klein, M. (1946). "Notes on some schizoid mechanisms". In: J. Mitchell (ed.) *The Selected Melanie Klein*. Harmondsworth: Penguin Books, 1986.

Klein, M. (1957). "Envy and Gratitude". In: *Envy and Gratitude and Other Works 1946–1963*. NY: Dell Publishing Co.

Klein, M. (1975). *Envy and Gratitude and Other Works 1946–1963*. NY: Dell Publishing Co.

Knights, D. and Morgan, G. (1993). "Organization Theory and Consumption in a Post-Modern Era". *Organization Studies*, 14 (2): 211–34.

Krantz, J. (1993). "The managerial couple: superior-subordinate relationships as a unit of analysis". In: L. Hirschhorn and C. Barnett, *The Psychodynamics of Organizations*. USA: Temple University.

Krantz, J. (1996). *Anxiety and the New Order*. Paper presented at the Annual Symposium of ISPSO at the Marriott Financial Centre, New York, (June).

Krantz, J. and Gilmore, T. (1990). "The Splitting of Leadership and Management as a Social Defense." *Human Relations*, 43 (2): 183–204.

Lacan, J. (1977). *Ecrits*. London: Tavistock Publications.

Lasch, C. (1979). *The Culture of Narcissism: American life in an age of diminishing expectations*. NY: Norton.

Lawrence, W.G. (1998). (ed.) *Social Dreaming @ Work*. London: Karnac Books.

Lawrence, W.G. (1998). "Won from the void and formless infinite". In: W.G. Lawrence (ed.) *Social Dreaming @ Work*. London: Karnac Books.

Lawrence, W.G. (1999). "Centring of the Sphinx for the Psychoanalytic Study of Organisations". *Socio-Analysis*, 1 (2): 99–126.

Lawrence, W.G. (2000). *Tongued with Fire: Groups in experience*. London: Karnac Books.

Lawrence, W.G. (2005). *Introduction to Social Dreaming: Transforming thinking*. London: Karnac.

Lawrence, W.G., Bain, A. and Gould, L. (1996). "The Fifth Basic Assumption". *Free Associations*, 6 (37): 28–55.

Levine, David P. (2005). "The Corrupt Organisation". *Human Relations*, 58 (6): 723–40.

Lewis, M. (1990). *Liar's Poker*. London: Coronet Books.

Long, S.D. (1991). "The Signifier and the Group". *Human Relations*, 44 (4): 389–401.

Long, S.D. (1992). *A Structural Analysis of Small Groups*. London: Routledge.

Long, S.D. (1993). "The Nature of Symptom Formation in the Individual and its Relevance to Other Human Systems". *Australian Journal of Psychotherapy*, 12 (1/2): 166–84.

Long, S.D. (1999). "The Tyranny of the Customer and the Cost of Consumerism: An analysis using systems and psychoanalytic approaches to groups and society". *Human Relations*, 52 (6): 723–44.

Long, S.D. (2000a). "Conflict and co-operation: two sides of the same coin". In: R. Wiesner and B. Millet (eds) *Current Issues in Organizational Behaviour*. Australia: Jacaranda Wiley.

Long, S.D. (2000b). "Engaging the Task: A socio-analytic discussion of task presence and absense". *Socio-Analysis*, 2 (1): 80–101.

Long, S.D. (2002). "Destructivity and the Perverse State-of-Mind". *Organizational and Social Dynamics*, 2 (1): 179–207.

Long, S.D. (2006). "This used to be my playground: family/work dynamics". In: A. Mathur (ed.) *Dare to Think the Unthought Known*. Tampere: Aivoairut Publishing, pp. 135–52.

Long, S.D. and Newton, J. (1997). "Educating the Gut: Socio-emotional aspects of the learning organisation". *Journal of Management Education*, 16 (4): 284–301.

Malkiel, B.G. (2003). *A Random Walk Down Wall Street: The time-tested strategy for successful investing*. NY: W.W. Norton.

Marcuse, H. (1955). *Eros and Civilization*. London: Sphere Books.

Marx, K. (1906). *Capital: A critique of political economy*. In 3 volumes edited by Fredrick Engles. Chicago, IL: Charles H. Kerr and Co.

McKendrick, N., Brewer, J. and Plumb, J. (1983). *The Birth of a Consumer Society*. London: Hutchinson.

Menzies-Lyth, I.E.P. (1970). *The Functioning of Social Systems as a Defence against Anxiety*. Tavistock Institute of Human Relations, Pamphlet No. 3.

Menzies-Lyth, I. (1988). *Containing Anxiety in Institutions*. London: Free Association Books.

Menzies-Lyth, I. (1989). *The Dynamics of the Social*. London: Free Association Books.

Miller, E.J. (1993). *The Vicissitudes of Identity*. Opening Address to the 3rd International Group Relations and Scientific Conference, Lorne, Victoria, Australia.

Miller, E. (1995). "The Healthy Organization for the 1990s". In: S. Long (ed.) *International Perspectives on Organizations in Times of Turbulence*. Melbourne: Swinburne University publication.

Miller, E. (1999). "Dependency, alienation or partnership? The changing relatedness of the individual to the enterprise". In: R. French and R. Vince (eds) *Group Relations Management and Organization*. Oxford: Oxford University Press.

Newton, J., Long, S. and Sievers, B. (eds) (2006). *Coaching in Depth: The organisational role analysis approach*. London: Karnac.

Nobus, D. (2006). "Locating perversion, dislocating psychoanalysis". In: D. Nobus and L. Downing (eds) *Perversion: Psychoanalytic perspectives*, pp. 3–18. London: Karnac.

Nobus, D. and Downing, L. (eds) (2006). *Perversion: Psychoanalytic perspectives*. London: Karnac.

Nossal, B. (2007). *Systems Psychodynamics of Consulting*. Unpublished Thesis.

Obold-Eshleman, Christa (2004). "Victims' Rights and the Danger of Domestication of the Restorative Justice Paradigm". *Notre Dame Journal of Law, Ethics & Public Policy*, 18: 571–603.

Ohmae, K. (1990). *The Borderless World: Power and strategy in the interlinked economy*. USA: McKinsey and Co.

Owen, Justice Neville (2003). "Report of the Royal Commission on the Collapse of HIH". Government Printer, Canberra.

Oxford English Dictionary

Pajaczkowska, C. (2000). *Ideas in Psychoanalysis: Perversion*. UK: Icon Books.

Peters, T. and Waterman, R.H. (1982). *In Search of Excellence*. New York: Harper and Row.

Pope, R. (2006). *Cultural Psychoanalysis, or Theory, Resurrected*. http://muse.jhu.edu/journals/theory_and_event/v009/9.1pope.html.

Puget, J. (2002). "Contributions from South America: From the group as jigsaw puzzle to the incomplete whole". In: R.D. Hinshelwood and M. Chiesa (eds) *Organizations, Anxieties and Defences: Toward a psychoanalytic social psychology*. London: Whurr Publishers.

Pusey, M. (1991). *Economic Rationalism in Canberra: A nation building state changes its mind*. Cambridge: Cambridge University Press.

Ragland-Sullivan, E. (1978). *Jacques Lacan and the Philosophy of Psychoanalysis*. Chicago, IL: University of Illinois Press.

Ralston Saul, J. (1997). *The Unconscious Civilization*. Harmondsworth: Penguin Books.

Ramsay, I. (2005). HIH – *The First Legal Scalps*, ABC Law Report, 19 April.

Rayner, C. and Hoel, H. (1997). "A Summary Review of Literature Relating to Workplace Bullying". *Journal of Community and Applied Social Psychology* 7: 181–91.

Rieff, P. (1959). *Freud: The mind of the moralist*. Chicago, IL: University of Chicago Press.

Rieff, P. (1966). *The Triumph of the Therapeutic: Uses of faith after Freud*. Great Britain: Penguin Books.

Robinson, P. (1969). *The Freudian Left: Wilhelm Reich, Geza Roheim, Herbert Marcuse*. NY: Harper and Row.

Rose, N. (1990). *Governing the Soul*. London: Routledge.

Rosenbluth, H. and McFerrin Peters, D. (1998). *In Good Company: Caring as fiercely as you compete: Lessons from America's best companies*. Addison-Wesley.

Rosenfeld, J.M. and Tardieu, B. (2000). *Artisans of Democracy: How ordinary people, families in extreme poverty, and social institutions become allies to overcome social exclusion*. Maryland, USA: University Press of America.

Salecl, R. (1998). *(Per)versions of Love and Hate*. London: Verso.

Schoeck, H. (1966). *Envy: A theory of social behaviour*. NY: Harcourt, Brace and World.

Sennett, R. (1998). *The Corrosion of Character: The personal consequences of work in the new capitalism*. NY: W.W. Norton and Company.

Sievers, B. (2000). "Competition as War: Towards a socio-analysis of war in and among corporations". *Socio-Analysis*, 2 (2): 1–27.

Sievers, B. and Mersky, R. R. (2006). "The Economy of Vengeance: Some considerations on the aetiology and meaning of the business of revenge". *Human Relations*, 59 (2): 241–59.

Slater, P.E. (1966). *Microcosm: Structural, psychological and religious evolution in groups*. NY: John Wiley and Sons.

Spicer, B., Emanuel, D. and Powell, M. (1996). *Transforming Government Enterprises*. CIS Policy Monographs 35. Queensland, Australia: The Centre for Independent Studies.

Stacey, R. (2001). *Complex Responsive Processes in Organizations: Learning and knowledge creation*. London and NY: Routledge.

Stack Sullivan, H. (1950). "The Illusion of Personal Individuality". *Psychiatry*, 13: 317–32.

Stein, M. (2000a). "The Risk Taker as Shadow: A psychoanalytic view of the collapse of Barings bank". *Journal of Management Studies*, 37 (8): 1215–29.

Stein, M. (2000b). "After Eden: Envy and the defences against anxiety paradigm". *Human Relations*, 53 (2): 193–212.

Stein, M. (2005). "The Othello Conundrum: The inner contagion of leadership". *Organization Studies*, 26 (9): 1405–19.

Stein, M. (2003). "Unbounded Irrationality: Risk and organizational narcissism at Long Term Capital Management". *Human Relations*, 56 (5): 523–40.

Steiner, J. (1993). *Psychic Retreats: Pathological organizations in psychotic, neurotic and borderline patients*. New Library of Psychoanalysis edited by Elizabeth Bott Spillius. London: Routledge in association with the Institute of Psychoanalysis.

Sullivan, H.S. (1950). "The Illusion of Personal Individuality". *Psychiatry*, 13: 317–32.

Sykes, T. (1994). *The Bold Riders*. St Leonards, NSW: Allen and Unwin.

Sykes, T. (2006). "Address to a Quadrant Dinner", published in *Quadrant*, May 2006.

Symington, J. and Symington, N. (1996). *The Clinical Thinking of Wilfred Bion*. London and New York: Routledge.

Taylor, B.E., Chait, R.P. and Holland, T.P. (1996). "The New Work of the Non Profit Board". *HBR* September–October 1996.

Wastell, D. (1996). "The Fetish of Techniques: Methodology as a social defence". *Info Systems Journal*, 6: 25–40.

Waterman, R.H., Waterman, J.A. and Collard, B. (1994). "Toward a Career Resilient Workforce". *HBR* July–August.

Weber, M. (1946). *Essays in Sociology*. Edited by H.H. Gerth and C. Wright Mills, Oxford University Press, UK.

White, S. (2001). "A Life Cycle Theory of Bullying: Persecutory anxiety and a futile search for recognition in the workplace". *Socio-Analysis*, 3 (2): 137–54.

Wikipedia, the free encyclopedia (2006). http://en.wikipedia.org/wiki/LTCM.

Willshire, L. (1997). *Psychiatric Services: Organising an impossible task*. Unpublished Ph.D. thesis, Monash University, Melbourne, Australia.

Winnicott, D.W. (1958). *Collected Papers: Through paediatrics to psychoanalysis*. London: Tavistock Publications.

Winnicott, D.W. (1971). *Playing and Reality*. London: Tavistock Publications.

www.applet-magic.com/ltcm.htm.

www.erisk.com/Learning/CaseStudies/ref_case_ltcm.asp.

INDEX